Organizing Your

Family History Search

Efficient & Effective Ways
to Gather and Protect
Your Genealogical Research

Sharon DeBartolo Carmack

BETTERWAY BOOKS
CINCINNATI, OHIO

About the Author

Sharon DeBartolo Carmack is a Certified Genealogist who writes a regular column in *Reunions* magazine. She is a frequent speaker at genealogy conferences and seminars and has appeared on the PBS television series *Ancestors*.

Other Books by Sharon DeBartolo Carmack

A Genealogist's Guide to Discovering Your Female Ancestors
The Genealogy Sourcebook
Italian-American Family History: A Guide to Researching and Writing About Your Heritage
Communities at Rest: An Inventory and Field Study of Five Eastern Colorado Cemeteries
The Ebetino and Vallarelli Family History: Italian Immigrants to Westchester County, New York

Organizing Your Family History Search. Copyright © 1999 by Sharon DeBartolo Carmack. Manufactured in the United States of America. All rights reserved. No part of this book may be reproduced in any form or by any electronic or mechanical means including information storage and retrieval systems without permission in writing from the publisher, except by a reviewer, who may quote brief passages in a review. Published by Betterway Books, an imprint of F&W Publications, Inc., 1507 Dana Avenue, Cincinnati, Ohio 45207. (800) 289-0963. First edition.

Other fine Betterway Books are available from your local bookstore or on our web site at www.familytreemagazine.com.

05 04 03 02 01   8 7 6 5 4

Library of Congress Cataloging-in-Publication Data

Carmack, Sharon DeBartolo
　　Organizing your family history search / Sharon DeBartolo Carmack.—1st ed.
　　　　p.　　cm.
　　Includes bibliographical references and index.
　　ISBN 1-55870-511-2 (alk. paper)
　　1. Genealogy. 2. United States—Genealogy Handbooks, manuals, etc. I. Title.
CS44.C375　1999
929′.1—dc21　　　　　　　　　　　　　　　　　　　99-21643
　　　　　　　　　　　　　　　　　　　　　　　　　　　　CIP

Editor: Roger D. Joslyn, CG
Production editor: Christine Doyle
Production coordinator: Erin Boggs
Designer: Sandy Kent
Cover designer: Stephanie Redman

To my father, Sal Bart, the most organized person I know.

Acknowledgments

Many friends and colleagues contributed organizing tips, and I am indebted to them all: Robert Charles Anderson, Gale Williams Bamman, Mary McCampbell Bell, Laurie Carmack, Ruth Herlacher Christian, Sharron Currie, Regina Hines Ellison, Robert Fineberg, Jonathan D. Galli, Duncan B. Gardiner, Jeffrey L. Haines, Laura DeBartolo Heidekrueger, Ge Lee Hendrix, Marty Hiatt, Kathleen W. Hinckley, Henry Z Jones Jr., Roger D. Joslyn, Elizabeth Kelley Kerstens, Suzanne McVetty, Marie Varrelman Melchiori, Elizabeth Shown Mills, David L. Mishkin, Marie Martin Murphy, Joy Reisinger, Marsha Hoffman Rising, Jean Rodwick, Christina K. Schaefer, Katherine Scott Sturdevant, Sharon Swint and Marcia Wyett.

My appreciation is also extended to several friends and colleagues who have yet to say no whenever I ask them to read drafts of my books. Their comments and suggestions were invaluable, as always: Roger D. Joslyn, Anita Lustenberger, Suzanne McVetty, Katherine Scott Sturdevant, Sharon Swint and Marcia Wyett.

Special appreciation is due Robert Charles Anderson for bringing Hugh Kenner's essay on untidy desks to my attention; and Rick W. Sturdevant, Ph.D., Senior Research Historian, Air Force Space Command History Office, Peterson AFB, Colorado, for providing longevity data on storage media.

Many thanks go to my editor Bill Brohaugh, at Betterway Books, for his ideas, suggestions and quick responses to my never ending barrage of questions by E-mail. Okay, Bill, so with revisions, maybe it took a little longer than six days.

Finally, to my husband, Steve, and daughter, Laurie, I owe my greatest appreciation for their tireless support.

\di'fin\ *vb*

Definitions

Genealogical Title Abbreviations Used in This Book

CALS	Certified American Lineage Specialist
CG	Certified Genealogist
CGL	Certified Genealogical Lecturer
CGRS	Certified Genealogical Record Specialist
FASG	Fellow, American Society of Genealogists

Icons Used in This Book

 CD Source — Databases and other information available on CD-ROM

 Definitions — Terminology and jargon explained

 For More Info — Where to turn for more in-depth coverage

 Idea Generator — Techniques and prods for further thinking

 Important — Information and tips you can't overlook

 Money Saver — Getting the most out of research dollars

 Notes — Thoughts, ideas and related insights

 Printed Source — Directories, books, pamphlets and other paper archives

 Quotes — Useful words direct from the experts

 Reminder — "Don't-Forget" items to keep in mind

 Research Tip — Ways to make research more efficient

 See Also — Where in this book to find related information

 Step By Step — Walkthroughs of important procedures

 Sources — Where to go for information, supplies, etc.

 Timesaver — Shaving minutes and hours off the clock

 Tip — Good ideas to keep in mind

 Warning — Stop before you make a mistake

Table of Contents At a Glance

Table of Contents

beyond the basics, preparing to write articles and books, and taking on projects from editing family newsletters to indexing record sources for other family historians.

Appendixes:

ONE

Why Genealogists Need to Be Organized

You need not feel embarrassed or alone. It has happened to all of us. Not a single genealogist alive or dead was prepared for the onslaught of *stuff* associated with tracking past lives. Sure, this pastime of yours probably began innocently enough with just one sheet of paper: a pedigree chart. And that one sheet of paper was capable of holding *so* much information: vital statistics on four or five generations of people. But at some point, and it's difficult to say exactly when, your one sheet of paper multiplied and divided. It added, but never subtracted. While you weren't looking, it called on its friends for company. All of a sudden, or so it felt, you became overwhelmed with paper. And photocopies. And books. And genealogical society newsletters. And maps. And correspondence. And computer printouts. And family photographs. And catalogs. And . . . and . . . and. . . .

THE GOALS OF ORGANIZATION

When I became interested in genealogy, my husband, daughter and I lived in a small, three-bedroom house. I did my genealogy at the kitchen table. Everything I needed fit neatly into one portable file box, so it was easy to get it out each day for work and put it away each evening for dinner. Today, we live in a large, six-bedroom house. My family hasn't grown; my genealogy has. I no longer use the kitchen table; I have my own "office." My genealogy also occupies part of a second spare room.

Now I'm certainly not suggesting you run out and buy a bigger house, although it *would* help. Since I know that's probably not a readily feasible option for most people, and because I know that no matter how much room

Quotes

A TEENAGER'S ORGANIZATIONAL METHOD

Sure, I'm organized. I have everything spread out on the floor of my bedroom, right where I can find things.

—Laurie Carmack

1

you have, it won't be enough, I will suggest ways to organize all of your genealogical matter—and *keep* it organized—in the space you do have or in the space you may not realize you have.

I also know that what works for one person may not work as well for another. What looks like an organizational method to one may look like complete chaos to another or feel like a straitjacket to a third. Since there are always several ways to do something, I have asked some of my friends and colleagues to contribute their organizational tips. Perhaps one of their methods, or a variation on one that I or they suggest, will suit your needs and circumstances.

The whole idea behind a good organizational method is to be able to find what you are looking for within seconds. Yes, I said *seconds*. You should not have to hunt for that death certificate on Uncle Johnny or that society newsletter with the article on how to obtain military records. You've already spent countless hours locating documents in the first place—in a courthouse, library, archive or attic. You don't need to spend even more time trying to find something again in your home.

SAVING TIME AND MONEY

Organization is about time. If you have lots of time on your hands, then you don't need to be organized. But if time is a valuable commodity, you need to be as efficient in your genealogical endeavors as you can be. Think how much more research and writing on your family history you could do if you were organized and didn't have to hunt for things. By being organized, you actually recover extra time you may have been wasting.

Organization is also about money. You may have saved for months so you could make that weeklong research trip to Washington, DC, or Salt Lake City. In that week, you accumulated a lot of new data. The following year, you decide to make another trip. If you haven't organized and recorded all that new data, you may end up wasting your money by duplicating your research. Or, if you weren't organized enough to get and record all that you needed the first time, you might end up returning to the same place instead of researching at another repository.

Money is also wasted if you haven't been organized and find yourself needing to hire a professional genealogist to take over a portion of your research. When one client engaged my services, it took me twenty-five hours to organize her materials before I could even begin researching. I had to know what had been done and what hadn't. Part of the problem was her husband: He had been happily entering all the data into a genealogy computer program and making printouts. None of the printouts had "revised as of" dates, so I couldn't tell which was the most recent printout. So along with creating a filing system for the client, I also had to compare and consolidate all of the computer-generated charts because the information varied so much from one chart to the next. I had him make a current printout, but in comparing it to previous printouts, some information was missing. It was a nightmare.

Several years after the client terminated research, she wanted to get back into genealogy. I was no longer taking clients then, so I referred her to a colleague. I had told my colleague that everything should be organized and ready to go, so she could pick up right where I had left off. The client, however, failed to show my colleague what I had organized and researched; it was months before the client finally found the research notebook I had created, but my colleague never did get to see the files I had created for the client. The client never bothered to show her.

THE SCOPE OF A GENEALOGY PROJECT

Organizing and genealogy go hand in hand. While I'm certainly no math wizard, it doesn't take much calculating to figure out that besides all of the documents and various sundries you will be collecting in the course of tracing your ancestry, you will also be collecting *people*—lots of them. If you trace back ten generations, you will be dealing with 2,046 ancestors. And that's just your ancestry. That doesn't count your collateral relatives: siblings, cousins, aunts, uncles and in-laws. It makes you feel overwhelmed just thinking about it, doesn't it? Yet you have to be able to keep track of everyone and the information on all of them. You also have to be able to stay on top of various projects you may be working on, and, if you are a professional genealogist, you also have all of your clients' ancestors to manage. I think I have tackled them all, too, at one time or another: organizing my own ancestral hunt; organizing research, writing and transcribing projects; and organizing clients' research.

After living for more than twenty-one years with an admittedly disorganized person (who shall remain nameless), I have learned that it is easier to *get* organized than it is to *stay* organized. I can help you become organized. I cannot keep you organized; that requires constant self-discipline. I can offer suggestions to boost that self-discipline. You will have to do the rest.

A FEW WORDS ABOUT YOUR GUIDE

Lest I come across as seeming flawless in my organizational methods, let me confess some of my more recent sins. I bought a book that I referred to often in one of my writing projects. It's William Dollarhide's *Map Guide to American Migration Routes*. For the longest time, I had no idea where I put that book. I looked everywhere. I'd never taken it out of the house, so it *had* to be there. It drove me crazy because I couldn't find it. And I knew as soon as I bought a second copy, I would find the first one. After hunting for months, I did find my copy. I had misshelved it on my bookcase, and because the spine is so thin and not titled, I couldn't easily see it. I had come very close to buying another one, however.

Tip

APPROACH ORGANIZATION A LITTLE AT A TIME

When my stacks of stuff get out of hand, my policy is to tell myself that by doing a little at a time, I can get it organized. It works, and I do get organized. And it always amazes me that I do.

—Ruth Herlacher Christian

Tip

GET ORGANIZED BY TAKING A TIME-OUT

I have made the most progress in solving time-management or organizational problems by taking at least one hour each week, sneaking off to a quiet location, and really thinking about one problem area. I usually try to pick one specific problem (e.g., the back table in my office is always overflowing with clutter). Rather than just resolving to "do better," I've found that it is very important to honestly evaluate the *reasons* a problem develops. I then can brainstorm a number of possible solutions and develop a set of goals to act on these solutions. Some of the culprits on my back table were catalogs that had not yet been "filed" in the horizontal stack of catalogs kept on a bookshelf. I eliminated this problem by storing catalogs and book fliers vertically in magazine storage boxes alphabetized by vendor/publisher. This example may seem absurdly simple, but I have found that nearly all of my time-management and organizational problems are made up of any number of such simple components. I only see them when I take the time to look, however.

—Jeffrey L. Haines, CG

Originally published in *Association of Professional Genealogists Quarterly* 10 (March 1995): 24.

I have stacks of paper in my office—four to be exact. This is actually an organizational method. The stacks are by project. I have a stack for the family history writing project I'm currently working on. I have a stack for the class I'm teaching. I have a stack for this book. And I have a small stack of correspondence that needs answering. I like to think they are *organized* stacks, and they are, for the most part. But, yes, there have been occasions when I've placed something in the wrong pile and had to sift through all the piles to find it.

Recently I was doing research at the Family History Library in Salt Lake City. I found one of my ancestors in the census. I dutifully copied all the information onto a census extraction form. Then, as I opened my file to place it in chronological order with other censuses on that family, guess what I found? An extraction of the exact same census I had just copied.

As I was preparing for another research trip to Salt Lake City, I knew I had a copy of a report from another genealogist *somewhere* in my files. I had cited it as a source on the project I'm currently researching. I even wrote "copy in the possession of the compiler"—me. I went through everything, twice. Three times. The next day I decided to look in a binder that was left over from a former organizational system (the binder method discussed in the next chapter). Sure enough, the report was there.

See, it happens to everyone, even to the authors of books on organization. Fortunately, these are the exceptions rather than the rule for me. And, no, my spices are not arranged in alphabetical order, and the clothes in my closet are not grouped by color. Even though my genealogy is organized and my office is relatively neat, the rest of my house hasn't been cleaned since . . . well, let's not get into that.

It is so easy to get overwhelmed, especially when you have several projects going at the same time. These could be your own research projects, projects for clients or projects as a volunteer for a genealogical society committee. And if *you* can get overwhelmed, think of what will happen to all of your materials when you die. Do you think your descendants will take the time—or be able—to organize your genealogy when you haven't? I think the only thing they will be organizing is a lovely bonfire.

GOALS OF THIS BOOK

In this book, we'll look at
- creating and maintaining filing systems
- preparing for research trips
- getting organized after one trip and before the next one
- organizing the various sundries you will collect besides research (books, catalogs, photographs, cassette tapes, computer disks and CD-ROMs, microforms, tombstone rubbings, maps—the list goes on and on)
- organizing research projects
- finding room in your house for all your genealogy stuff
- moving your genealogy materials when you move into a new home
- organizational methods for professional genealogists
- organizing and preserving your genealogy for your descendants

Forms and Computer Organization

In this book I'll discuss forms for various tasks **(blank forms for you to freely reproduce appear starting on page 134)**. I'll be honest with you; I'm not big on forms. I use only a few of them. Like many genealogists, I find most forms too limiting, with never enough space to write what I want to write. It is also a lot cheaper to condense many forms' worth of notes onto notebook paper or my laptop computer than to reproduce forms and carry stacks of them with me. Not to mention the more forms you have, the more paper you have to keep track of and organize. But if you feel forms would better suit your needs than notebook paper, then by all means, use them. If the ones included in this book don't suit you, adapt them and design your own.

While I will discuss, to some degree, organizing data (information on your ancestors), there are plenty of forms, charts, books and computer software programs available to help you with that. **If you need help, you may want to consult**
- *The Unpuzzling Your Past Workbook* by Emily Anne Croom
- *Managing a Genealogical Project* by William Dollarhide

Sources

For More Info

I cannot recommend one computer genealogical software program over another because, frankly, I don't even use one, but some of the more popular ones are Family Tree Maker, Ultimate Family Tree, The Master Genealogist, Personal Ancestral File (PAF) and Brother's Keeper. By the way, the reason I don't use one is that I don't want to spend time entering years of research into a computer program. I'd rather spend my time doing more research. I began in the days when people were still using those things called typewriters. However, I do use a computer and its word processing program, which allows for greater flexibility in manipulating and formatting data.

Office Supplies

I have tried to use common names for office supplies so you can easily ask for them or find them in the index of an office supply catalog for a national chain, such as Viking, Office Max, Office Depot and Staples. While the name of an item may not ring a bell, once you see it, you'll recognize it. Actually, if the name of an item isn't familiar to you, then you may not have the gene that stimulates organization. This is a recessive gene that compels you to thumb through office supply catalogs for pleasure. **You can also find many office supply items at less cost through discount department stores, such as Kmart, Wal-Mart and Target. Shop around.** Watch for those back-to-school sales and tax-time sales. These are excellent opportunities to stock up on office supplies. You'd be amazed at how inexpensively you can organize and outfit your genealogy nook or office if you shop around.

THE ORGANIZATION QUIZ

You may already be more organized than you think. Perhaps there is an organized person hiding somewhere in you. To find out, take this little quiz:

- Do office supply stores give you the same thrill you had as a kid when you walked into a toy store?
- Do you find yourself distracted from what you really need to do by the urge to reorganize something that would make it easier to do the task you're supposed to be doing?
- Do you like to color code things, such as files?
- Do you compulsively straighten your desk or table before and after you begin working on your genealogy?
- Do you micro-organize, so that, for example, you have subfiles within files?
- Do you worry that you should be better organized?
- Is your office supply catalog your favorite book to read for fun and relaxation?
- Does it make you crazy not to have everything you need at your fingertips?
- Do you buy and read books about organizing?

If you answered yes to *any* of these, then I can assure you that you're

Money Saver

For More Info

ORGANIZATIONAL HELP FROM THE PROS

For those who are organizationally challenged, I suggest you contact the National Association of Professional Organizers for more help than I can provide: NAPO, 1033 La Posada Dr., #220, Austin, TX 78752-3880; phone: (512) 206-0151; fax: (512) 454-3036; E-mail: napo@assnmgmt.com; Web site: www.napo.net.

already on the brink of being organized, perhaps even compulsively so. If not, you will be after reading this book.

I know the word *organization* can send chills down the spines of the most respected and intelligent people. I walk into a disorganized space only to run out in tears because it's so overwhelming. Still, it can be done. I promise I'll guide you through every step of the dreaded way.

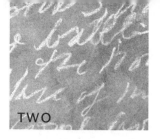
Creating and Maintaining a Family History Filing System

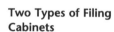our filing system is the heart of your genealogical research. Finding details about your ancestors may quicken your pulse, boost your adrenaline and make you feel giddy with success, but if you can't easily retrieve that data once you've already collected it, you aren't going to feel the same exhilaration tracking it down again—even though you may spend just as much time and energy finding it the second time.

THE BASICS OF FILE STORAGE

There are, of course, some bare necessities you will need regardless of the filing system you decide to use:
- filing crates, boxes or cabinets
- file folders
- file labels (optional)

Filing Crates and Cabinets

If you are just starting out in the genealogical world, it is economical to begin with plastic filing crates or plastic file boxes you can find at office supply stores or discount department stores. (And they come in so many neat colors now.) Your research files should never go with you on a research trip—they stay at home for safekeeping—so this should not have a bearing on your decision on which type or color of file to buy. When you get to the point of filling two or more crates or file boxes, it's probably time to purchase a two-, three- or four-drawer vertical filing cabinet. Discount department stores are generally less expensive than office supply stores when it comes to buying a filing cabinet, but make sure the construction is sturdy and the drawers slide in and out easily. Around the first of the year (in preparation for inventory and tax-preparation time), many stores put filing cabinets on sale. Office supply stores (both local and mail order) sometimes

Two Types of Filing Cabinets

Vertical file cabinet

Lateral file cabinet

offer free delivery when you spend a certain dollar amount.

Lateral filing cabinets cost more than vertical ones, but they also hold more and provide space for office equipment. A standard, vertical filing cabinet extends from the wall about 18″ (45.7cm); a lateral filing cabinet extends about 14″ (35.6cm). But lateral filing cabinets are generally 42″ (106.7cm) wide and take up more wall space; a vertical cabinet is 15″ (38.1cm) wide. Naturally, you will stack things on top of the filing cabinet (why waste space?); a lateral one is large and sturdy enough to hold books, a compact photocopy machine or a computer printer.

Fire-safe filing cabinets are extremely costly and heavy, but you may consider them worth the investment, given the material you will be storing in them. There will be heirlooms and other items that you will want to protect for future generations (see chapter ten). Frankly, I think there are other ways to preserve your research, however, such as publishing it or making it widely available. The majority of what you will keep in your working files could, with some effort, be reconstructed if it were lost in a fire, flood or other natural disaster. No one wants to face that monumental task—so do your best to avoid losing everything—but it is cost prohibitive and nearly impossible to store everything relevant to your genealogy in fire-safe cabinets.

If you have small children or grandchildren occupying your home, consider purchasing locking filing cabinets. It might be a wise idea to lock your

Tip

ORGANIZING WITHIN A FILING CABINET

I keep various types of genealogy in different file cabinet drawers. My late husband's family documents and files are in one, my present husband's are in another, mine is in a third and my clients' research is in the fourth. I keep old client files in a small file cabinet, but I am planning to trim down these files soon and put them in a storage box for safekeeping but easy access.

—Regina Hines Ellison, CGRS

Tip

ADVICE ON USING FILING CABINETS

I recently switched from a standard filing cabinet to a vertical filing cabinet, which takes up less room in my small office. The top shelf holds active files, maybe fifty or so, and the bottom holds files of more permanent interest, such as reference materials, long-standing client files and personal family history data and correspondence.

There is a central core of files that is well organized, and then there is another periphery of chaotic files that, for some reason, my psyche does not want to permit into the organized group. Some are active now, this week, this month; others beg for attention in some other way, and I fear putting them away too well.

Case files older than two years are put in Bankers Boxes in the storage room. This generally only happens when the top file drawer gets too full. I have another indexing system, on computer, keyed to client reports, which lets me track the same families to some extent.

—Duncan B. Gardiner, Ph.D., CG

Originally published in *Association of Professional Genealogists Quarterly* 10 (December 1995): 116.

USING HANGING FILE FOLDERS

I never wanted to use hanging folders because I like to pack and carry folders as I work on projects. Then, when my files became numerous enough to fill several cabinets, I became annoyed with the tendency of simple manila folders to slouch into oblivion in file drawers. I now use hanging file folders in cabinets to keep separate matters that I must organize by folders. They never slouch, but glide freely regardless of my moving them about. Their upright labels are much easier to spot and read and do not wear out easily. Hanging, box-bottom file folders are perfect if the contents are thick.

I still use standard file folders to pack and carry lecture notes and portable projects. I switched to using purple rather than beige folders, however, to make being organized more pleasant by treating myself to my favorite color.

—Katherine Scott Sturdevant, historian

genealogy files while they are around to prevent little hands from coloring lovely pictures on your documents, cutting paper dolls out of Great-Grandma's diary or gluing Great-Uncle Paul's Civil War pension record together. Chances are they will also have little regard for your filing system and could considerably shuffle your research.

File Folders

At the same office supply or discount department stores, you should also purchase at least one box of one hundred letter-size file folders to get started. They are cheaper to buy in bulk, and I promise they won't go to waste. **Avoid legal-size anything.** Both legal-size files and filing cabinets are a lot more expensive, and frankly, unnecessary. You will have a variety of paper sizes to deal with anyway, so you may as well take the more economical route.

File folders now come in a variety of colors, and if those colors had been available when I began my filing system, I would have color coded it. Now it would be a waste of time and money to redo my filing system just to have colored file folders. You may choose one color file folder for your maternal line, one for your paternal line, one for your spouse's maternal line and one for your spouse's paternal line. Another color file folder can be used for genealogical society information, forms and charts, client files or items pertaining to localities.

File Labels

File labels are optional unless you are using hanging file folders. You may choose to write directly on the folder tabs (using different colors of ink, if you want to color code inexpensively), or you can make classy looking labels on your typewriter or computer (and with color printers, you can color code that way, too). **Using color file labels is more economical than buying file folders in different colors.** I use blue file labels for my paternal lines, red for my maternal, yellow for my husband's paternal lines and green for his maternal.

FILING SYSTEMS

There are probably as many different filing systems as there are genealogists, but each has one aspect in common: ancestors. Every genealogist is collecting material on ancestors. What genealogists do with that material is another story. Ideally, your research note-taking should revolve around whatever filing system you establish so items are easily filed and retrieved after each research trip. I'm going to discuss several different methods of filing, along with potential problems of each, if any. It doesn't matter what system you use, as long as it's easy for you to set up, use and *maintain*.

The Binder Method

Some genealogists use the binder method. For every surname on their pedigree charts, they have a separate binder. Family group sheets, pedigree charts and photocopies of documents are all three-hole punched and placed neatly in the binder. The binder goes with them on research trips, so they have all the data readily accessible. Obviously, if the surname extends back to colonial times or further and includes research on collateral lines, the binders will be quite bulky and cumbersome to lug around. If you are planning a lengthy research trip to work on several families, you will have quite a few binders to carry with you. **While this may be a good starting system, it becomes impractical quickly.** Don't get me wrong; binders do have their place, which I'll discuss in later chapters.

Filing by Surname

Similar to the binder method, some genealogists use one file folder per surname. This method uses the least amount of folders, but they will become obese in no time at all. You will quickly have "PACKARD Family, Volume 1," "PACKARD Family, Volume 2," etc., and you will be sifting through many papers to find the one item you need. I generally start with this method, then as I gather more material on a surname, I subdivide the documents into a filing system by surname and the type of record, discussed later in this chapter.

Filing by Surname and Locality

This is an extension of the surname filing system, only you subdivide the surname by places where you are researching: "PACKARD: Massachusetts," "PACKARD: Illinois." Or you can further subdivide it by towns or counties: "PACKARD: Boston, MA," "PACKARD: Kankakee Co., IL." This method is more useful if you also include on your file labels the years in which the family was in that locality: "PACKARD: Kankakee Co., IL, 1860–65." One of the limitations of this method is that if several generations stayed in the same locality for decades, this system suffers from the same problem as when you file simply by surname.

Filing by Individuals

Remember in chapter one, I said that if you research ten generations you'll be gathering material on 2,046 people? That does not take into consideration the collaterals: aunts, uncles, cousins, in-laws. If you have unlimited space for an unlimited amount of filing cabinets and folders, filing by individuals would be a good method. Ever glance at the filing cabinets in your doctor's office? This will give you a good idea of the space you will need if you go with this system. Come to think of it, you probably have more ancestors and collaterals than your doctor has patients, so you'll need even more room. You'd also be duplicating for filing a lot more source material that refers to two or more people—more so than with any other system. Filing by individuals would be perfect, however, if you were planning to write a biography of one individual. Otherwise, skip it.

Filing and Note-Taking by Couples or Family Groups

This system is better than the individual filing method and is a popular filing system among genealogists since it coordinates with the couples listed on a pedigree chart. Start by making a family group sheet (see page 15) for every married couple listed on your pedigree chart. Then create a file folder for each couple and their offspring. When you learn that a child married, you start a file folder for that person and spouse. If a son or daughter never married, then that child's data stays in the file folder of the parents. This system, like others, has the potential of becoming unwieldy. If a couple had several children who did not marry, you will have to hunt in an overly voluminous file folder.

Label file folders with the couple's names, using the maiden name for the wife: "Christopher C. GREGORY and Mary STUART." Also add their ID numbers from your pedigree chart. Most pedigree charts use the *ahnentafel* system. This numbering system works on the principle that every ancestor is assigned an identifying number. After the individual whose pedigree is charted, men are given even numbers; women, odd. On your pedigree chart, you would be number 1; your father, number 2; your mother, number 3. In the **ahnentafel**, which, by the way, is German for "ancestor table," you can double a person's number to get the father's number and double a person's number and add one to get the mother's number. So, for example, your father is number 2 on your pedigree chart. Doubling his number, you get his father (your paternal grandfather), who is number 4. Add one, and you get your father's mother (your paternal grandmother), who is number 5. The same would be true for your mother's parents. Her number is 3. Her father is 6; her mother is 7.

Combine the individual identifying numbers from your pedigree chart

Tip

ORGANIZING USING "MASTER" FOLDERS

For the ancestors I am researching, I use a "master" folder with the name of the person I am researching. In this folder, I have subfolders. Each one of these is headed with a topic, e.g., passenger list, draft registration, censuses, city directories, etc. This gives me some semblance of order and seems to work. It is a lot of work, however, and sometimes I run into problems. For instance, I may have to make several copies of a document if it applies to more than one person, such as a passenger list that has more than one family member on it.

—Robert Fineberg

\di'fin\ *vb*

Definitions

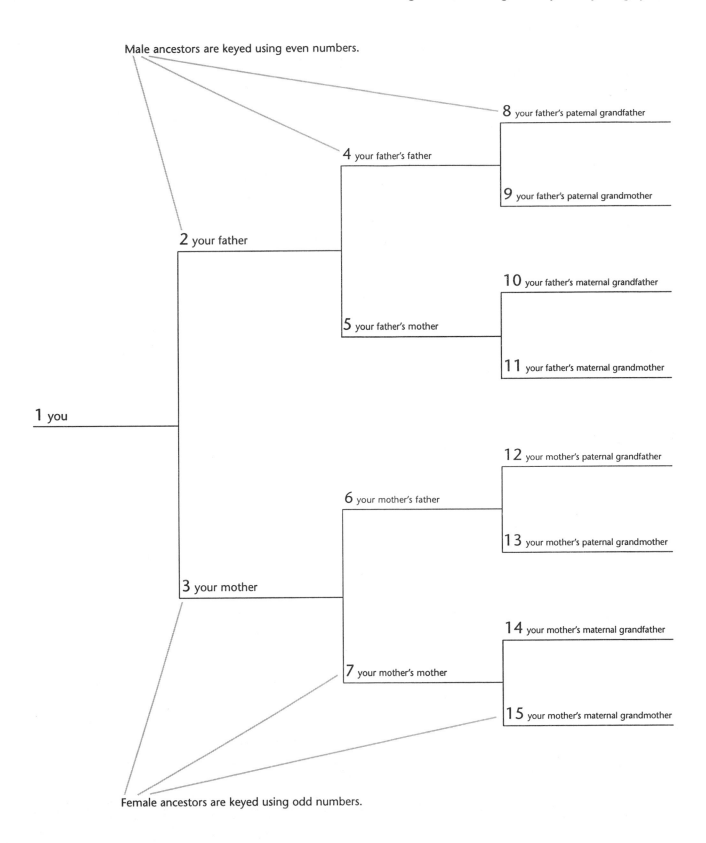

Male ancestors are keyed using even numbers.

8 your father's paternal grandfather

4 your father's father

9 your father's paternal grandmother

2 your father

10 your father's maternal grandfather

5 your father's mother

11 your father's maternal grandmother

1 you

12 your mother's paternal grandfather

6 your mother's father

13 your mother's paternal grandmother

3 your mother

14 your mother's maternal grandfather

7 your mother's mother

15 your mother's maternal grandmother

Female ancestors are keyed using odd numbers.

Pedigree chart showing *ahnentafel* numbering system

for the couple to number the group sheets and your file folders. For example, Joseph DeBartolo is number 4 on my pedigree chart. Stella Ebetino, his wife, is number 5. Their combined number is 4/5. This is the number I'll use on their family group sheet and their file folder's label. Arrange your files in numerical order and use your pedigree charts as your index. Some people put only the number on the file label, but numbers to me are meaningless. I need numbers *and* names. On the outside of the file folder, list the names of the children for this couple so that you can find this information easily.

Please **do not try to invent your own numbering system!** No numbering system is perfect; they all have some kind of flaw. It is best to use one that other genealogists will recognize when you share your research.

When you learn that a child married and you create a file folder for that couple, the number you assign will be based on the parents' combined number, unless that child is your ancestor. (In that case, the child will be on your pedigree chart and already have an assigned number.) Let's look at an example. Suppose there are three children for couple 4/5 (your paternal grandparents):

> i. John
>
> ii. Susan
>
> iii. Charles

Say John is your father, and he appears as number 2 on your pedigree chart. When you create a file for John and your mother, the number they will have on their file folder is 2/3, his number and your mother's number. Now, Susan is not on your pedigree chart because she is not your ancestor; she's a collateral relative. The same goes for Charles. If they each married, give them the following numbers: Susan (and her spouse), 4/5ii; Charles (and his spouse), 4/5iii. This tells you that their parents are couple number 4/5 and the Roman numerals give you the birth order. (Or you could number them 4/5.2 or 4/5.3. It doesn't matter as long as you're consistent.)

TABLE OF CONTENTS FOR FILES IN THE COUPLE OR FAMILY GROUP FILING SYSTEM

Typically, organizing and finding documents within a folder is easy. In each couple's folder, you keep a copy of the family group sheet up front, which serves as a table of contents, so to speak. In the upper right corner of the family group sheet, place the corresponding identification numbers from your pedigree chart. Also on the family group sheet, you should be citing your sources of information. For each piece of data on the family group sheet, you assign a footnote number. If you are working with a handwritten chart, circle these numbers so they are distinguishable from dates or other numbers on the chart. On the back of the sheet, or on an attached sheet when you run out of room, you list by corresponding footnote number the

Warning

Tip

FILING BY PEDIGREE CHART NUMBERS

My files are numbered according to corresponding numbers on my ancestor/ pedigree chart, not by names. In order to find the appropriate number for a person, I have an alphabetical database and a reference sheet in the front of the file cabinet. I also keep a file by surname for all of the miscellaneous information that doesn't fit into any exact ancestor's file. I have two sets of family group sheets; one in the file and another working set in a binder that I take with me when I'm researching.

—Laura DeBartolo Heidekrueger

FAMILY GROUP SHEET

ID #8/9

> Combined identifying numbers for husband and wife from numbers on pedigree chart

Husband: Catlett Conway FITZHUGH

Born: 25 Apr 1831① ②   Place: King George Co., Va.① ②

Married: 27 Nov 1860 ①   Place: Madison Co., Va.①

Died: 22 May 1908 ② ③   Place: Green Co., Va.③

Buried: Place: Old Fork Episcopal Church Cemetery, Hanover Co., Va.②

Parents: James Madison FITZHUGH and Mary Fitzhugh STUART ①

Wife: Ellen Stuart CONWAY

Born: 31 Aug 1837① ②   Place: Madison Co., Va.① ②

Died: 6 Mar 1912②   Place: Louisa Co., Va.④

Buried: Place: Old Fork Episcopal Church Cemetery, Hanover Co., Va.②

Parents: Battaile Fitzhugh Taliaferro CONWAY and Mary Ann WALLACE ①

Children: ⑤

> Circled footnote numbers reference sources of informations

etc.

---

1 Madison Co., Va., Marriage Register 1:12, FHL 32595.

2 Tombstone inscription, Old Fork Episcopal Church, Ashland, Hanover Co., Va.

3 Obituary, *The Daily Progress* [Charlottesville, Va.], 27 May 1908.

4 Oral history interview with Louise Fitzhugh, Gordonsville, Va., 12 Oct. 1985.

5 1870 Census, Virginia, Greene Co., Standardsville, p. 75, #519-510; 1880 Census, Virginia, Greene Co., Standardsville, ED 59, p. 9, #80-80; 1900 Census, Virginia, Hanover Co., Beaver Dam Dist., ED 20, sheet 21 B, #405-414.

The family group sheet is used as a table of contents when filing by couple or family group.

full source citation of the document which supplied you with the data. **(See chapters four on page 39 and chapter six on page 63 for more on documentation.)** If you are using a genealogy computer software program, the program should automatically assign the reference numbers for you.

Behind the family group sheet, arrange your documents in the file according to the footnote numbers. Let's look at an example. On the Family Group Sheet above, each piece of information is given a footnote number, which corresponds to the document from which that piece of information came. Use these numbers as page numbers on the actual supporting documents, whether they are photocopies or your notes. For instance, all the data with footnote number 1 came from Madison County, Virginia, Marriage Register, volume 1, page 12, on microfilm at the Family History Library in Salt Lake City, Utah, film number 32595. I made a photocopy of the record for

See Also

my files. On the photocopy, in the upper right corner, I write a number 1. It gets filed right behind the family group sheet. To further identify the record in case it gets separated from the file, in the upper left corner of the document put the couple's identification number that corresponds to the family group sheet.

During a visit to the Old Fork Episcopal Church in Ashland, Virginia, I copied tombstone inscriptions on my notes. After recording the information on my family group sheet and giving it the next footnote number, I also put this number on the upper right corner of my notes and filed them behind the photocopy of the marriage record.

When I received a copy of the obituary, I followed the same procedure, giving it the number 3. And so on.

When I want to see a document in this filing system, I merely scan my footnotes or look at the data and the corresponding footnote number per the family group sheet. Then I can easily find the document since it is labeled with that number and filed in numerical order.

NOTE-TAKING AND CROSS-REFERENCING

You will want to take notes according to your filing system for ease in maintaining it and for this system to work properly. Use a separate sheet of paper or form for each couple or family group (**see the Note-Taking Form: Couple or Family Group Filing Method on page 18**). Even if you are taking notes on one or more children of the couple, put the *couple's* name and ID number on the page, since this is how you will file your notes.

If a document or your notes also cover someone other than the couple or their children, still cite the information on your family group sheet and give the data the next footnote number. If you are going to file the document in another couple's file, either make a photocopy or add a sheet of paper showing the source citation, your footnote number and a notation cross-referencing the document to the other file.

For example, you have a deed in which Thomas Benton Montgomery is selling land to Reuben McMasters. You can photocopy or abstract the deed and place one copy in the Thomas Benton Montgomery and wife file and one copy in the Reuben McMasters and wife file. Or, you can put the deed in the Thomas Benton Montgomery and wife file, then make a cross-reference sheet for the Reuben McMasters and wife file. Here's how it works: First note the information from the deed on your Thomas Benton Montgomery and wife family group sheet. Then assign the information a footnote number and cite the source on the family group sheet. Put the footnote number on the upper right corner of the deed and file it numerically with the other documents behind this family group sheet.

In the Reuben McMasters and wife file, follow the same procedure of recording the information on the family group sheet, assigning it the next footnote number and citing your source on the family group sheet. Instead of having the deed to file, however, you are going to use a sheet of notebook

A Useful Form You Can Reproduce
For a full-sized blank copy of the Note-Taking Form: Couple or Family Group Filing Method, see page 134. You are free to photocopy this form for personal use.

paper. On the paper, write the deed's citation, and use the footnote number you used on the Reuben McMasters and wife family group sheet as your document number. Write "See Thomas Benton Montgomery and wife file, document number —, for a copy of the deed."

The problem you will have with note-taking is when you are photocopying several pages, say from a book of cemetery transcriptions, that list several individuals and families. It may not be practical to make copies of all the pages for each couple's folder. In that case, you may want to make a locality folder and put the cemetery transcriptions in it, along with other similar documents that pertain to multiple families living in the same area.

For example, I'm researching the Shough family of Patrick County, Virginia. I have file folders for five Shough couples and their offspring and one for a Shough daughter who married a man with the surname Gregory. In a book of cemetery transcriptions for Patrick County, I photocopied a dozen pages that pertained to Shoughs and Gregorys. I made a file folder labeled "Patrick Co., Va." In it, I put the photocopies of the cemetery transcriptions and notes I took when searching deed indexes for all the Shoughs and Gregorys who owned land in Patrick County. Then, I put a note cross-referencing these items in each of the six file folders on the couples.

I mainly use the system of filing by couple or family group when I am working on certain projects, such as a three- or four-generation study. Otherwise, I prefer the next system.

Filing and Note-Taking by Surname and Record Type

Files in the surname and type of record filing system are labeled "DeBartolo: Census," "DeBartolo: Land Records," "DeBartolo: Immigration Records." If I am looking for a census enumeration on Albino DeBartolo that I've photocopied or abstracted, I merely need to go to the file labeled "DeBartolo: Census." This system also grows with your research and is customized to each family. For instance, you don't need a file labeled "DeBartolo: Military Records" if you have not sought these types of records or if no one in the DeBartolo family served in the military.

Typically, you are researching by record type, and ideally, you will take your notes accordingly. It makes sense to keep your filing system following that same line of thinking. If you take notes based on your filing system, then when it comes time to put away all of your research when you get home, it will be an easy, stress-free, preorganized and, therefore, less time-consuming process. Let me show you how this system works.

I'm looking for land records in Orange County, Virginia, for two surnames: Fitzhugh and Stuart. From the deed index, I copy all the entries for Fitzhugh onto one sheet of paper; all the entries for Stuart go onto another sheet. (See page 21 for a sample page of notes.) Suppose I am using a microfilm copy of the index from a Family History Center (a local "branch" of the main Family History Library in Salt Lake City) and at a later date will need to order microfilms of the deed books, or I may need to request copies directly from the Orange County courthouse. I can take my notes of the

Warning

DANGER: PAPER CLIPS AND STAPLES

I do not recommend paper clips in files. First, they fall off or hold hands with other clips or other papers when they are not supposed to, or they may snag and tear papers. Second, in humid areas at least, they will rust over time and stain your papers. If you insist on using them, get the plastic-coated kind.

Staples are also a problem, even though they are better for keeping papers together. They, too, will rust over time and may snag or tear papers. Best to use them for short-term stuff (papers you will later toss).
—Roger D. Joslyn, CG, FASG

Page ___1___ of ___1___

Date __5 Feb. 1999__

NOTE-TAKING FORM
Couple or Family Group Filing Method

Couple _Catlett C. Fitzhugh and Ellen S. Conway_   File Number _8/9_

Type of Record _Marriage_

Title/Source _Madison Co., Va., Marriage Register, 1793-1905_

Condition of Record _good, easy to read_

Author/Editor/Compiler_____

Publisher_____

Place & Year of Publication_____

Volume_1_   Page number_12_   Call #/Microfilm # _32595_

Repository _Family History Library, SLC_

Notes/Abstract

Marriage, 27 Nov 1860, Madison Co., Va., License dated 10 Nov 1860

Fitzhugh, C.C., age 29, single, born King George Co., Va., resides Richmond

parents: J.M. Fitzhugh and M.F. Stuart

occupation: merchant

and

Conway, Ellen, age 22, single, born Madison Co., Va., resides Madison Co.

parents: B.F.T. Conway and M.A. Wallace

no witnesses listed

Thos. L. Ho [unreadable], Minister of the Gospel

Note the slight difference between the form on this page (which would be filed according to couple or family group) and the form on the opposite page (which would be filed according to the surname and record type being researched). On this form, you must key the notes to the couple's I.D. number

For blank copies of both these forms that you can photocopy for personal use, see pages 134 and 135.

Page _1_ of _1_
Date _5 Feb. 1999_

NOTE-TAKING FORM
Surname/Type of Record Filing Method

Surname _Fitzhugh_   Type of Record _Marriage_

Title/Source _Madison Co., Va., Marriage Register, 1793-1905_

Condition of Record _good, easy to read_

Author/Editor/Compiler_____

Publisher_____

Place & Year of Publication_____

Volume _1_   Page number _12_   Call #/Microfilm # _32595_

Repository _Family History Library, SLC_

Notes/Abstract

Marriage, 27 Nov 1860, Madison Co., Va., License dated 10 Nov 1860
Fitzhugh, C.C., age 29, single, born King George Co., Va., resides Richmond
parents: J.M. Fitzhugh and M.F. Stuart
occupation: merchant
and
Conway, Ellen, age 22, single, born Madison Co., Va., resides Madison Co.
parents: B.F.T. Conway and M.A. Wallace
no witnesses listed
Thos. L. Ho [unreadable], Minister of the Gospel

As noted elsewhere, on each new page of notes (not just on forms like these), record the following information:
- the surname you're researching
- the date you're doing the research
- the repository where the information was found
- complete source citation—including county, state, book volume, page(s), microfilm number (if pertinent)
- the condition of the record or microfilm (for example, "too dark," "out of focus," "faded," "water-stained," "torn," "out of order," "tight binding")

Tip

ORGANIZING YOUR RECORDS ON COMPUTER

You're packing for the research trip of a lifetime, and you need to have access to all of the research you've already done. But you don't want to take reams of paper with you on your trip, so what do you do?

A solution is to use a computer program called Clooz—the electronic filing cabinet for genealogical records. Clooz is a database built on a Microsoft Access platform. It is *not* a lineage-linked database, but rather is a tool to assist you with your research and with organizing your records.

If your filing system is simple, there is a greater likelihood that you will continue to maintain it. The more difficult and time-consuming your filing system, the more likely your records will continue to pile up in your in box. While there are several different ways to file records, I have found that filing them by record type is the most flexible system.

If you're planning a research trip, you'll find Clooz useful for both the preparation and for the journey. Before you go, enter the records you have on the family you will be researching. The templates allow you to give each entry a unique number, enter in information specific to that entry, and link the people you've found in the entry. You click on the individual's detail button to enter information specific to that individual, including the name as it appears in that record.

By having this information on my laptop while I am researching, I can avoid duplication and easily see where I have holes in my research. While I'm at repositories, I use Clooz along with a research calendar to keep track of every source I look at and the results of the search.

Census information storage is the most popular feature of Clooz. In addition to the various federal census formats, there is also a generic "head of household" census form and a generic form for all members of a household. These generic forms are useful for state or local censuses or censuses in foreign countries (some foreign census forms are included in Clooz).

For More Info

For more information on Clooz, visit the Web site at http://www.ancestordetecti ve.com. Or write to Ancestor Detective, P.O. Box 1457, Drawer C, Woodbridge, VA 22193-1457. Clooz requires Windows 95 or 98.

—Elizabeth Kelley Kerstens, CGRS

Adapted from her article "Finally—Help for Organizing Your Records!" *Roots Users Group of Arlington, VA Newsletter* 10 (January 1998): 925-28.

index entries and file them accordingly (or keep the entries in my research notebook, discussed in chapter four). The Fitzhugh index entries go into the file folder labeled "FITZHUGH: Land Records"; the Stuart index entries are filed in the "STUART: Land Records" folder.

Once I have access to the actual documents or microfilm copies, I'm going to look up each entry and make abstracts **(see chapter four, page 39)** or photocopies, grouping all the Fitzhugh abstracts together. When I abstract the Stuart entries, I will begin a new sheet of paper. I do not abstract a deed for a Fitzhugh onto the same paper that also has an abstract for a Stuart, since they will go into two different files. All notes pertaining to the Fitzhugh deeds are on their own sheets, and the same for the Stuarts. When I get home, I can easily file the notes.

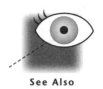

See Also

Fitzhugh   15 Apr 1998
                                         Family History Library, Salt Lake City

Orange Co., Va., Deeds, General Index, 1800–92, vols. 2–3, FHL 33010

*Fitzhugh, Jas. M. from Winslow, Henry B., deed 36:67, 23 Oct 1835

*Fitzhugh, Jas. M. from Powell Fielding, deed 36:401, 26 June 1837

*@Fitzhugh, Mary F. from Fitzhugh, Jas M., deed 39:258, [can't read date]

*Fitzhugh, Mary F. from [unreadable], Michael, deed 40:99, [can't read date]

*Fitzhugh, [blank] from Barbour, B.J., et al., deed 43:420, 29 Aug 1855

ƒFitzhugh, F.C. from Tisdale, J.B., trust 54:544, 3 Sept 1892

*@Fitzhugh, Mary F. from Marshall, Thos A., trust 45:329, 29 Jan 1861

ƒFitzhugh, Mary F. to Peers, Alunda J., deed 48:535, 27 Dec 1873

ƒFitzhugh, Mary F. from Marshall, Thos. A., trust 48:636, 18 Mar 1872

@ made abstract

* made photocopy

ƒ need to order from Orange Co., not on film at FHL

An example of note-taking organized according to surname and type of record. This sample represents my notes as I searched for land records. Note that even though I was looking for two families, this page contains notes for only one of the two. These entries go into a file labeled "FITZHUGH: Land Records"; the others, in a file labeled "STUART: Land Records." Notice that I mark my notes with symbols to identify the entries I abstracted or photocopied and those I need to request by mail.

A Useful Form You Can Reproduce

For a full-sized blank copy of the Note-Taking Form: Surname/Type of Record Filing Method, see page 135. You are free to photocopy this form for personal use.

Reminder

Whether or not a form is used, the heading of every new page of notes has the following information (**see the Note-Taking Form: Surname/Type of Record Filing Method on page 19**):

- surname being researched
- date of research
- repository
- complete source citation, e.g., county, state, deed book volume, page(s), microfilm number (if pertinent)
- condition of the record or microfilm (for example, "too dark," "out of focus," "faded," "water-stained," "torn," "out of order," "tight binding")

So what happens when a deed pertains to both a Fitzhugh and a Stuart, where one is buying land from the other, for instance? You have two options: (1) make a duplicate of your notes and put one in the FITZHUGH: Land Records file and one in the STUART: Land Records file, or (2) put the notes in one file and a cross-reference, such as See FITZHUGH: Land Records, in the other file. This dilemma will come up for other records, too, such as marriage documents, census enumerations (with more than one surname in the household or on the same page or in the same town) and cemetery transcriptions, to name a few. Handle these in the same manner.

Taking notes from cemetery transcriptions and censuses brings up another point. Whether you go to the cemetery or are copying information from a published transcription of the cemetery, **you need to preserve the order (unless it's alphabetical) in which you find the names.** The same is true when you copy information from a census. You need to know that the Fitzhughs lived next door to the Stuarts. And you need to know that the plot behind James Fitzhugh's grave is that of a Stuart, since this could mean a family connection. In this instance, taking notes with one surname per sheet of paper can defeat your research goals. In these cases, I would copy *in order* all the information on the relevant surnames together and make one photocopy of the notes for each pertinent surname file.

CHOOSING FILE NAMES

Here is a sampling of types of records or label headings you might use. Simply add the surname prior to the record name:

- birth records
- cemetery records (or further subdivide: cemetery records; funeral home records)
- census
- church records (or breakdown further: baptism records, meeting records, etc.)
- city directories
- court records
- death records

Tip

MORE ON COMPUTER FILING

My biggest challenge has been trying to organize in excess of twenty-five years of family research into a logical order and then computerize it. My system was by family, but it got completely out of control. When I heard of Clooz, the electronic filing cabinet, I decided to give it a try.

It was without a doubt the best thing I have ever decided to do, after marrying my husband. Getting documents ready to enter into Clooz has made me reread and rethink what I've collected. By reorganizing in a record or document method, I'm quickly picking up where there is a missing piece in my research.

I'm locating many cases of duplicated efforts in separate family folders. The documents are now being arranged by type, e.g., birth, marriage, death, census, land, city directories, etc. Being able to link a person to a document and then display the records will make research trips much more organized. I can list all the documents connected to a person or all the people connected to a document.

Although this is just in the beginning stages, I am feeling, at long last, that I am in control of my records—not that they control me.

—Marie Varrelman Melchiori, CGRS

- divorce records
- family correspondence
- immigration (or further subdivide: passenger lists; naturalization records)
- land records
- marriage records
- military records (or subdivide by name of war: Revolutionary War, Civil War, etc.)
- newspaper items
- obituaries
- probate (wills, inventories, etc.)
- published genealogies/articles (If you have quite a bit of published material on a surname, it may work better to three-hole punch the photocopies and place them in a separate binder labeled accordingly.)
- school records
- tax records

File alphabetically by surname, then type of record. If you are color coding by maternal and paternal lines, file all of the maternal lines alphabetically, then by record type, the same as you did for the paternal files.

TABLE OF CONTENTS FOR FILES

Surname_____*DeBartolo*_____   Record Type_____*Obituaries*_____

Enc.#	Date	Listing of Search	Repository/Address	Source Citation	Results	Date Rec'd	Money Sent
3.	15 Mar	Joseph DeBartolo, d. 1	Daily Item, 33 New	1 Aug 1929, p. 11	received	1 May 1998	none
			Chester,		photocopy		
1	15 Mar 1998	John DeBartolo, d. 19 Mar 1943	Greenwich Library, 101 W. Putnam Ave., Greenwich, CT 06830	Greenwich Times, 19 Mar 1943, p.2	received photocopy	6 Apr 1998	none
2	15 Mar 1998	Albino (d. 2 Oct 1946) and Lucia DeBartolo (d. 22 Jun 1940)	Sutro Library Genealogy Section, 480 Winston Dr. San Francisco, CA 94132		Library does not have newspapers after 1899. Try Calif. State Library in Sacramento.	10 Apr 1998	none
4 also see Ebetino enc. 8.	23 Apr 1998	Stella (Ebetino) DeBartolo, d. 5 Aug 1981	Daily Item 33 New Broad St. Port Chester, NY 10573		nothing found	12 May 1998	none

Annotation on table: **Enclosure or page number of document within file folder. Numbers are assigned in the order in which documents are acquired, no requested**

Annotation on table: **Cross-reference notation to another file where the same information can be found**

Table of contents used with the filing system by surname/record type.

TABLE OF CONTENTS FOR FILES IN THE SURNAME/ TYPE OF RECORD FILING SYSTEM

Although categorizing your files by surname and record type will organize everything and help you find needed documents quickly, there is one more part of each file that will allow you to retrieve documents within seconds: the table of contents (see the Table of Contents for Files above). You may recognize the table of contents as similar to a search calendar or log.

Here's how it works: Each file will have its own table of contents page(s). In the upper left, enter the surname to which the contents pertain. In the upper right, enter the type of record. This information corresponds with the file's label.

Step By Step

When you send away for a document, record the date, the ancestor for which the search was made (you know what kind of record it was because of the file it's in, e.g., obituary, birth record, probate), the repository and address where you wrote and the amount of money (if any) you sent. Essentially you are duplicating and simplifying the information in your request letter. This form is similar to a correspondence log, but it goes a little further because it will keep track of more than correspondence.

When you acquire a document by mail, assign it a page number (or enclosure number) for your files. Put the number somewhere on the front of document, such as the upper right or left corner. Also record on the table of contents the rest of the information:

- the complete source citation
- the results of your request
- the date you received an answer to your request

Also note if you needed to send a follow-up letter ("Did you get my initial request?").

If you are returning from a research trip where you obtained the records yourself, fill in all the columns when you file the documents.

Each document you obtain and file will be given the next consecutive page/enclosure number. This number may be out of sequence on your table. For example, let's say you wrote for three documents on the same day and listed them on your table (minus the page number and the results). Suppose you received a response to your second request before the others. This response is the first document to arrive, so it gets page/enclosure number 1. Now suppose a response to your third request arrives next. It will be page/enclosure number 2. When you finally get a response to the first request, it will be page/enclosure number 3.

The order of the page numbers on the table of contents is not important. All documents will be in numerical order in the file folder. It is important that the Listing of Search column be as uncluttered as possible, listing mainly the name of the person for whom you are searching. When you want to find the obituary for John DeBartolo, you simply glance down that column for his name. The Results column will tell you if you have it or need to get it from another repository, and the Enc. column will give you the corresponding page/enclosure number so you can quickly find it in your file.

I file my documents with the most recently acquired one first, right after the contents page, so page/enclosure number 1 is at the back of the file folder. You may decide you would rather file them in the opposite direction, with the most recently acquired documents in the back and number 1 at the front. Either way will work. Just be consistent in all of your files.

If you have a document that pertains to two surnames, choose one surname under which to file the document. Then in the other surname file's table of contents, enter the document as you did in the first file, except under enclosure/page number add a cross-reference notation. Suppose the document is a marriage record. File the document in the groom's file

A Useful Form You Can Reproduce
For a full-sized blank copy of the Table of Contents for Files form, see page 136. You are free to photography this form for personal use.

OVERVIEW AND COMPARISON OF POPULAR FILING SYSTEMS

Filing by Couple or Family Group

CREATING FILE FOLDERS

- Every couple on your pedigree chart gets a file folder, as needed.

- Label the folder with the names of the couple (wife's maiden name) and the combined ID numbers of the husband and wife from your pedigree chart.

- List names of the couple's children on the outside of the file folder for quick reference.

- If a child married, make a file folder for that marriage. If the child is an ancestor, use the number from the pedigree chart. If the child is collateral, use the parents' ID numbers with numerals added to indicate birth order.

- File numerically by couple number (husband/wife).

TABLE OF CONTENTS AND FILING

- Use the family group sheet on a couple as the table of contents for the couple's file.

- Record data on the family group sheet, cite sources of data on the back or an attached sheet and assign each piece of information a footnote number.

- Assign the same footnote number to your notes or the photocopy of the document that gave you the information.

- Behind the family group sheet, file the document numerically in the file according to footnote numbers.

- If a document pertains to more than one family, make a photocopy for the other family's file or cross-reference using a sheet of notebook paper.

Filing by Surname and Type of Record

CREATING FILE FOLDERS

- Create file folders for surname/record type combinations, as needed.

- Label folders with the surname, followed by the type of record, e.g., McMasters: Obituaries or McMasters: Census Records.

- Arrange file folders alphabetically by surname then alphabetically by type of record.

TABLE OF CONTENTS AND FILING

- Use a table of contents form at the beginning of each file folder.

- Record data on the family group sheet, cite sources of data on the back or an attached sheet, assigning each piece of information a footnote number. Then enter all the data (date, listing of search, repository, source citation, results, etc.) on the table of contents. The family group sheets are kept in your research notebook.

- Assign the document or your notes the next consecutive enclosure or page number for that file folder.

- Note the enclosure or page number on the document, and file it numerically in the folder.

- If a document pertains to more than one family, make a photocopy for the other surname's file or cross-reference in the Enc. # column of the table of contents.

OVERVIEW AND COMPARISON OF POPULAR FILING SYSTEMS (Cont'd)

NOTE-TAKING

- Take notes according to your filing system.

- Use a separate sheet for each couple or family group, labeled according to the filing system.

- If notes pertain to more than one family, either make a photocopy, cross-reference, or begin a file folder for the locality and cross-reference to it.

NOTE-TAKING

- Take notes according to your filing system.

- Use a separate sheet for each surname and record type, labeled according to the filing system.

- If notes pertain to more than one surname, either make a photocopy, cross-reference, or begin a file folder for the locality and cross-reference in surname folders.

(FITZHUGH: Marriage Records), then make the same notation in the bride's file (CONWAY: Marriage Records), but in the enclosure/page number column, write a cross-reference ("see Fitzhugh, enc. 4").

CHOOSING A FILING SYSTEM

If you are just starting in genealogy, you are probably overwhelmed already just trying to decide which filing system to use. An overview of both popular systems is on page 26.

If you're still unsure of which system you think you would like better, try both. Use the filing method by surname and type of record for one surname; try the filing method by couple or family group for one or two families. See which one suits you, or use a combination of both, like I do. My overall filing system is by surname and type of record. When I am working on a project with three or four generations, I create files by couples or family groups. This works for me. Do what works for you.

THREE

Oh No! Not *More* Files!

Y ou thought you were done, didn't you? Sorry. There's more. Once you have your basic filing system in place, there are other items that need filing, so you will need to create more files. Isn't this fun?

HANDLING AND FILING CORRESPONDENCE

There isn't a genealogist alive who doesn't write letters. When you're starting in genealogy, it seems you live for the arrival of the letter carrier. (If the mail carrier is of the opposite sex, your spouse may wonder if there's something more going on than mail delivery!) You no longer buy a few stamps at a time; you buy a roll of one hundred. Not only are you writing millions of letters, you're including a self-addressed stamped envelope (SASE) with every request. You write letters to family members, "genealogy" cousins (those related but several times removed from the ancestor you have in common), courthouses, libraries, vital records offices, cemeteries and archives. If you are being a good and true genealogist, the post office has displayed your picture, right next to the "Most Wanted" posters, as its most valued customer.

The more you write, the more you accumulate reams of paper: copies of letters you've sent, responses to letters you've sent, lists of letters you've sent, lists of letters you need to write, letters you've received from people you've never heard of who want copies of everything you have on the Jones family.

In the old days when I began genealogy (that would be just fourteen years ago), the only way to correspond was via the post office. Today you can also E-mail and fax your letters. Because it is so quick and easy to communicate with others, you may actually have more correspondence to handle today than you would have a few years ago. How can you manage it all?

You must stay on top of correspondence because it can get out of hand quickly. When you receive a letter, after reading it through, highlight or

Important

Tip

SETTING UP A CORRESPONDENCE SYSTEM

When you begin organizing, the first question should be "Where should I put this?" If you are not blessed with ever increasing file cabinets, some alternatives are to collect or buy boxes. Moving boxes you assemble yourself (12"×16") and the boxes that reams of paper are sold in are sizes that fit regular file drawer measurements for letter-size documents. Hanging file holders will fit on the rim of these boxes, and you are in business to organize your file folders.

One common way to file is by alphabetizing by the person's last name. This method has stood the test of time. Thirty years ago, I color coded with colored labels and wrote the names on the labels. Years later the glue had dried and my labels were falling off. So I think a more lasting solution is to use alphabetizing along with color coding by marking a dot of color with a highlighter or Magic Marker. This opens up the possibility of identifying categories within your genealogical files such as different surnames, places, stages, etc.

When you are just beginning, you can have broad categories of folders, and as the material collects, you will need to make special folders for the people with whom you correspond more frequently by giving each of them their own folder listed by their last name, then first name. I file from back to front with the oldest correspondence in the back and in chronological order, filing the original letter and reply together. When you receive a letter, it is helpful to pen in a top corner the date you received it. Sometimes personal letters do not have dates on them. If there is a very pertinent item in a letter that you want to flag so it is easy to find, use a 1½"×2" self-stick note on the top file edge and label it. This becomes a movable tab that you can label and can save time in locating specific information you need to have at your fingertips.

Some individuals use folders for "inquiries sent," inquiries received" and "letters to answer" to temporarily store current material they are working on. As the answers are sent or received, they can then be shifted to more permanent folders.

Most important is to design a plan for organizing your correspondence and stick to it. Keep a paper trail by making copies of all letters and E-mail you send and receive.

—Jean Rodwick, Ph.D.

underline any part of the letter that requires action: a question to be answered, information to be sent, a comment to make. Then put the letter in a "to be answered" file or basket. When you sit down to write letters, you will not have to wade through the whole letter again. You can zero in on the part that requires you to do something. If your schedule permits, allow some time daily to handle mail. If you have a job outside of genealogy, then set aside time at least once a week to write and respond to letters and to *file* them.

Step By Step

Requests for Records

Let's start with record requests. You can handle organizing and filing requests in one of several ways. You can create a "correspondence pending" file for each surname. When you write to a repository inquiring about a record or requesting a copy, file a copy of the letter here.

Here's how it works. Suppose you write for a copy of a will on Isaac Montgomery. Put a copy of the letter requesting the will in a file labeled "MONTGOMERY: Correspondence Pending." In this file you may want to keep a list or correspondence log so you can quickly see what letters are outstanding, but this is only necessary if you are writing many letters for the Montgomery family. If you are only writing a few, there is no need to have a log or a list. Why create another piece of paper if you don't really need to?

After you have written the letter, also pull the MONTGOMERY: Probate file, if you are filing by surname and type of record, and enter the request on the table of contents. If you are filing by couple or family group, you can skip this step. When you receive a response, either discard the copy of the letter in the MONTGOMERY: Correspondence Pending file or file it and the response in the MONTGOMERY: Probate file. Finish filling out the information on the table of contents. Don't forget to enter the new data on your family group sheets regardless of the filing system.

If you are using the system of filing by couple or family group, create correspondence pending files by surname. When you receive a response, log the new information on the appropriate family group sheet, assign it a footnote number, put the footnote number on the response and file it numerically.

A second method of filing correspondence does not involve a correspondence pending file. Instead, keep copies of your outstanding letters in the appropriate file: A request for a will goes in the MONTGOMERY: Probate file; a request for a cemetery record goes in the MONTGOMERY: Cemetery Records file. Requests are still recorded on the table of contents. For the couple/family group filing system, put the letter in the file of the couple to which the letter pertains. You will also need to keep a correspondence log in each file. The problem with this method is that to see what requests are outstanding, you must search through many files. By having a correspondence pending file for each surname, you can quickly see what outstanding requests you have for that surname.

A third method is to have one huge correspondence pending file for everything. You will definitely need some kind of correspondence log, of course, so you don't have to sift through many copies of letters to see what's outstanding. **On page 137 is a sample log you can use** for this method or with correspondence pending files by surname.

A Useful Form You Can Reproduce

For a full-sized blank copy of the Correspondence Log—Research Requests form, see page 137. You are free to photocopy this form for personal use.

Here's an overview of the first method of handling correspondence based on your basic filing system:

OVERVIEW OF HANDLING CORRESPONDENCE

Filing by Couple/Family Group
SENDING A REQUEST FOR RECORDS

- Create a SURNAME: Correspondence Pending file.

- If writing many letters, keep a correspondence log in the file.

- Keep a copy of each request in the SURNAME: Correspondence Pending file.

Filing by Surname/Type of Record
SENDING A REQUEST FOR RECORDS

- Create a SURNAME: Correspondence Pending file.

- If writing many letters, keep a correspondence log in the file.

- Keep a copy of each request in the SURNAME: Correspondence Pending file.

- Record the request in the appropriate SURNAME: Record Type file's table of contents, e.g., the MONTGOMERY: Probate file for a request for a will.

AFTER YOU RECEIVE A RESPONSE

- Pull the appropriate couple/family group file folder.

- Record and document the new data on your family group sheet.

- Assign the next footnote number to the new data, and put this number on the response.

- File the response numerically.

- Either pitch the request copy filed in the SURNAME: Correspondence Pending file or file it with the response.

AFTER YOU RECEIVE A RESPONSE

- Record and document the new data on your family groups sheet kept in your research notebook.

- Pull the appropriate SURNAME: Record Type file.

- Finish filling in the table of contents based on the response, and assign the document the next page/enclosure number.

- File the response numerically.

- Either pitch the request copy filed in the SURNAME: Correspondence Pending file or file it with the response.

Even though you may save letters on your computer, keep a binder of model or form letters. Write across the top of the sample letter "Request for Death Certificate," "Request for Obituary," "Request for Land Records," etc., and the name of the computer file in which you saved it. When you need to write a letter, you can glance through your binder for the suitable one.

Letters to Relatives

For both basic filing systems, create a separate file for each surname labeled "SURNAME: Family Correspondence." All outgoing and incoming letters with genealogical information on a particular surname go in these files. **Use a**

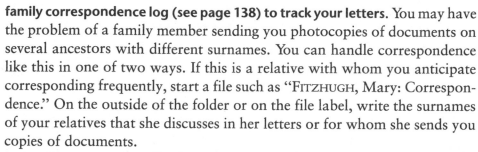

A Useful Form You Can Reproduce

For a full-sized blank copy of the Family Correspondence Log form, see page 138. You are free to photocopy this form for personal use.

Step By Step

family correspondence log (see page 138) to track your letters. You may have the problem of a family member sending you photocopies of documents on several ancestors with different surnames. You can handle correspondence like this in one of two ways. If this is a relative with whom you anticipate corresponding frequently, start a file such as "Fitzhugh, Mary: Correspondence." On the outside of the folder or on the file label, write the surnames of your relatives that she discusses in her letters or for whom she sends you copies of documents.

Another way to handle this situation is to file the relative's letter in the Fitzhugh, Mary: Correspondence file, making a list of the documents she sent to accompany the letter. Then put the documents in their appropriate files. Suppose, for instance, Mary sent you a copy of a will on Samuel Hooe, a copy of Martha Randall's death certificate and a copy of Francis Conway's Civil War pension. Note on the back of all these documents that you received them from Mary, citing her full name and address and the date you received the items. Then pull the Hooe: Probate file, enter the data on the file's table of contents, including that you received the copy from Mary, and file it. Do the same for the other two: Martha Randall's death certificate gets filed in the Randall: Death Records file, and Francis Conway's pension will be filed in the Conway: Military Records file.

If you are filing by couple or family group, you would note on the back of all these documents that Mary had sent you each item. Then simply file the documents in the appropriate couple's file folders. Note the new information on your family group sheets, assign a footnote number, cite your source, then file the document numerically.

If, however, a relative sends you photocopies of historical documents, such as several pages from a diary or a collection of papers about a particular ancestor, put these in a separate file labeled "Documents on Samuel Hooe from Mary Fitzhugh." Include in the file a sheet recording Mary's address, the date she sent the copies and whether she has the originals or how she acquired the copies. It would be a good idea to also note this on the backs of the documents, just in case they get separated from the file.

Here's an overview of how to file items you receive from family members.

If you receive a

Letter from relative with information pertaining to one family/surname:
a) Record information on family group sheet and cite source.
b) File under the appropriate couple/family group or in a Surname: Family Correspondence file.

Letter from relative with information pertaining to more than one family/surname:
a) Record information on family group sheets and cite source.
b) Make photocopies and file in each couple/family group file or in each Surname: Family Correspondence file; or

c) File in one couple/family group file or one Surname: Family Correspondence file, then make cross-reference notations as described in chapter two; or

d) Create a file labeled "[Name of the Relative]: Correspondence," and file the letter in it.

Letter from relative with photocopies of several documents pertaining to one family/surname:

a) Note on the backs of the documents from whom you received them and when.

b) Record information on your family group sheets and cite source.

c) If filing by couple/family group, place in appropriate file.

d) If filing by surname/type of record, file documents according to the surname to which the documents pertain and the type of record. Also create a file labeled "[Name of the Relative]: Correspondence," and file the cover letter and a list of documents that came with the letter in it.

Letter from relative with photocopies of several documents pertaining to several families/surnames:

a) Note on the backs of all documents from whom you received them and when.

b) Record information on your family group sheets and cite source.

c) If filing by couple/family group, place documents in files that correspond to the couple or family group.

d) If filing by surname/type of record, file documents according to the surname and the type of record to which each document pertains.

e) Create a file labeled "[Name of the Relative]: Correspondence," and file the cover letter and a list of the documents that came with the letter in it.

Letters to Write File

I often think of letters I need to write when I don't have the time at that particular moment to write them. Keep a single "letters to write" folder with a few sheets of notebook paper in it; you don't need a fancy log or chart for this one. When you think of a letter you need to write, jot it down in your file. The notation can be as simple as "Write Aunt Gabriella and ask if she has a copy of her father's death certificate" or "Send Uncle Richard a thank-you note for the photographs." Or the notation can be more detailed: "Write to the Nebraska State Historical Society to see if they have a collection of papers on Rev. Paul Mitchell (1882–1945). Also ask if they have any information on his family or the church he ministered for. If not, where can they direct me to write next?" As you write the letters, place a check mark and date in the margin or merely cross it off your list. File a copy of the letter and any response as described above.

Computer Filing for Correspondence

You do not need to rely solely on a paper method of filing your correspondence. Since you may be generating requests on your computer, keep computer files of letters you write. You can create computer "folders" or subdirectories for various types of correspondence: family correspondence, vital records requests, etc. Likewise, when you receive a response, you can either scan the letter into your computer for filing, or abstract or transcribe the response, then throw away the original. Before throwing any letter away, however, consider whether the original letter may have intrinsic value, such as the handwritten expressions of an earlier generation. **Remember to back up all computer files on a separate disk.** Also keep in mind that we don't know yet the true life of computer files and disks. Good quality paper we know can last for several generations, but we don't know whether changes in technology will render our computer file data inaccessible.

FILES FOR OTHER ITEMS

A client loaned to professional genealogist Gale Williams Bamman all her files pertinent to the case Gale was to handle. They were labeled with headings such as "Possibly Our Family," "Not Ours" and "The Mystery Man." While these may be adequate identifiers to you, if another genealogist ever needs to take over your research—because you've hired a professional or you have died—these headings probably won't be meaningful to anyone else. They may not even be meaningful to you ten years from now.

You will gather in the course of your research and through correspondence items that won't pertain to your family or that you don't immediately know whether they pertain to your family. In other words, you will likely gather material on someone with the same surname as one of your ancestors, but you aren't sure if that person is related to you. You can either designate that information to a separate file, such as "FITZHUGH: Relationship Undetermined" or "FITZHUGH: Iowa Branch," or you can file it with your other records and note somewhere on the document that the relationship to your family is uncertain or does not belong to your branch. I create a separate file using that individual's or couple's names: "DEBARTOLO, Michele: No Known Relation." The point is to clearly specify what's different about this file or record to remind you at a later date or for the benefit of the next person to work with your records.

You will also gather information pertaining to the locality where you are researching: foldable maps, materials on repositories, background research on the area, genealogical society information, and so forth. Make file folders with the locality's name: "Orange Co., Virginia," "Carroll Co., Arkansas" or simply "Connecticut."

ORIGINAL DOCUMENTS

Do not file any original documents in your files. By *original*, I mean precious, rare, fragile, historical documents. If you have Grandpa's original birth

Reminder

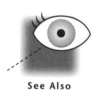

See Also

FOR FURTHER DISCUSSION

See chapter ten starting on page 115 for more on preservation and media longevity.

Tip

HANDLING BITS OF PAPER

I have for each state file folders where I file letter-size information received from state libraries, state archives, genealogical and historical societies, maps and lecture handouts. Then when I am researching in that state, I can refer to the file for helpful material.

Occasionally, the information about state records comes in little bits and pieces. Maybe a lecturer combined data about several states on one page of a handout, or there is mention in a society's newsletter about a new record a member discovered or a change of address for a repository, etc. Little bits of paper get lost in file folders or fall out. To keep these little bits of information from getting lost, I bought a 4″ × 6″ file box. I made tab dividers for every state from index cards and Avery labels. Then on index cards I glue or tape these small bits of information. I find it quicker and better to glue or tape than to take the time to recopy onto the index cards. Then as I research and find new books, films or other sources, I add this information to the index card.

—Marcia Wyett, CGRS

certificate or a letter written by Great-Aunt Mabel or Uncle Henry's discharge papers or your great-grandfather's naturalization certificate, make photocopies for your files. Handle the original items as infrequently as possible.

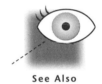

See Also

HANDLING VARIOUS PAPER SIZES IN YOUR FILES

FOR FURTHER DISCUSSION

Chapter ten, starting on page 115, discusses preserving historical documents.

If you've been using a steno pad, note cards, envelopes, napkins, sticky notes or scraps of paper for your notes, transfer them all now to 8½″ × 11″ paper (either by hand, photocopying or scanning) and throw the original away—unless, of course, the scrap has some inherent value, such as the family tree you drew on a paper napkin when you were ten. From now on, when you take notes, use either lined paper (and not spiral bound, unless the pages have a perforated left edge; otherwise the edges get caught on other pieces of paper when you tear them out), or if you are using a laptop computer, print out notes on 8½″ × 11″ paper. Little scraps of paper get lost too easily. In writing this book, I broke my own rule and proved this. I was away from home and thought of some items to include in the book. I jotted them down using the tiny notepad the hotel provided. When I came home, I stuck the pieces of paper in my file. They have fallen out at least six times!

While you can control the size of your paper for note-taking, you cannot always control the size of incoming paper, e.g., when a clerk makes a copy for you. The goal is to have all papers in your files the same size: 8½″ × 11″. If the page is larger than 8½″ × 11″, reduce the print size on a photocopy

USE SEPARATE FOLDERS FOR SPECIAL TOPICS

As you venture into maintaining family history files about the background social history in order to write family narrative, your file categories will change. The documents that you use will tend to be lengthier and may require separate folders. For example, my family history files go by titles such as

- HARPER, Kate: Transcript of memoirs

- SCOTT, James: Memoirs, chapter one

- DICKEY, Otho: Civil War experiences

- GATES, Wayne: Oral history transcript

- KANSAS: History of Sherman County (unpub. ms.)

- KANSAS: Articles on pioneer life

—Katherine Scott Sturdevant, historian

machine so that it fits on a letter-size sheet. Or you can fold it. It's okay; you can do it. Remember, this is not an original, historical document. It is a photocopy. If the paper you've acquired is smaller than 8½"×11", either photocopy it onto a letter-size sheet or attach it to one, if you want to preserve the original. You can also scan the document into your computer and make a working printout.

Every rule has an exception. That chatty letter from Aunt Martha with all the neat family history information will one day be an original, historical document. Unfold it if it's folded. Photocopy it for your files. Put your page/enclosure or footnote number on the copy. Do not bend, fold, staple or mutilate the original in any way, shape or form. This is the next generation's historical artifact. You may want to preserve it according to the methods discussed in chapter ten.

WHEN TO FILE

Being organized requires constant attention to filing and putting things away. When you let letters and research pile up, you can feel overwhelmed and take forever to get back on track. Regardless of whether you are a full-time genealogist or a part-time one, organization has to become part of your routine. I try to file and unclutter my desk daily as the mail arrives. This is the only way I can stay on top of all the paper in my office. Ongoing projects and frequently used items relating to a project are never put away until the project is complete, however. These items are straightened after use and kept within reach, either in a stack or a filing crate designated for that project. Granted, a professional genealogist may have more paper to deal with. But even a hobbyist, if an active member of a local genealogical society, will have more than personal family history research to cope with.

When I am gone for a ten-day research trip, it usually takes me at least a day or two to get caught up on the correspondence that has accumulated (mail, E-mail, faxes, telephone messages). It takes me about a week to update my sheets with the new findings and file the material I've accumulated on the trip. I won't even go into how much time it takes to catch up on laundry, housecleaning, sleep, etc.

I've heard the rule that you should only handle a piece of paper once. And in the course of holding that piece of paper, you have to decide whether to act on it, file it, pass it on to someone else for action or throw it away. Good in theory, hard in practice. This is where my stacks come in.

Items that need attention, whether they require a response or filing, stay on my desk where I can see them and where they will nag me until I do something about them. I really do dislike stacks, so that keeps me motivated to keep the piles to a minimum. Professional organizers will tell you to put these items in a tray or a file marked "to do" or some other such label, but I find that I consistently follow the "out of sight, out of mind" rule. So I keep the items in sight. Once again, this is a personal preference. Do what you can live with.

PURGING YOUR FILES

Your filing system never goes with you on research trips. It waits patiently for you to return. It happily grows fat with new material. In fact, it would be content to grow as obese as you would let it. But like the human body, a fat filing system is not a healthy one. It needs regular purging. Right now, mark a yearly or biannual date on your calendar as the day you will go through your files and eliminate unnecessary paper. This is also a good time to divide fat research files into two or more. I may start with one surname file on a family, but as it grows, it will need to be divided into surname/record type files.

If you find you are dreading the date you have marked as Purge Day, then clean out your files as you use them. Whenever you pull a folder to file or check something, take a minute to flip through the contents to see if anything can be tossed.

Purging files can be a lot of fun and beneficial to your research. As you purge, you will stumble across documents and letters you didn't remember receiving. And because your knowledge changes, you may discover something in one of the documents that you had overlooked the first time you saw it. With this in mind, even though for the most part your research files are probably fine and you need not purge items from them, it's still a good idea to pull each one and refresh your memory on what is there.

The other files you've created—for genealogical society meetings and seminars, for various articles, for localities where you need to do research or

Tip

USING BINDERS TO FILE INFORMATION ON STATES

I use a series of binders, arranged alphabetically by state. In the front of each state binder is a general information section with materials on state libraries, archives, vital records, etc. If I have a lot of stuff on counties, such as for New York, then each county has a section (alphabetical). Folded maps and small items go in pockets (you can purchase these three-hole punched with pockets on each side). If the item is small, I often photocopy it onto an 8½"×11" sheet and three-hole punch it. I prefer the binders with the clear plastic covers, so I can easily laser print labels for them and slip them in (and easily update them as necessary).
—Roger D. Joslyn, CG, FASG

Tip

CONTROLLING THE SIZE OF THE SHEETS IN YOUR FILES

There's nothing wrong with taking research notes on the backs of envelopes—but if you do, you must take all your notes on the backs of envelopes, and only on the backs, and all the envelopes must be of the same size.

When I tackle a folder of notes on a person or a family and odd-shaped scraps of paper fall out of the folder or get lost among larger-sized sheets of paper, my work is seriously impeded. Shuffling through and analyzing data on several sheets of paper is much easier if all the paper is of one size, with notes on one side only. And keep notes on different families on different sheets of paper.

—Robert Charles Anderson, FASG

for other miscellaneous items you have acquired—may need some trimming, however. The problem with purging files is sometimes you don't know what you will need in the future. My father taught me to throw away things after a year if I hadn't used or needed them. Genealogy, however, requires a different guideline. I have used for a research problem or to prepare a lecture materials and information that I hadn't looked at in five years, and I'm always glad I didn't throw them away.

You will have to be your own judge as to what you need to keep and what can be tossed. One way to make it easier is to put a "discard after" date on items you know you can throw away after awhile. For example, suppose you receive a flyer about a new genealogy book that you may want to purchase at a later date. You file it in your "Books to Buy" folder. Before you do so, put in big print at the top a "discard after" date, say, six months after you received the flyer. You can safely discard the flyer after that date because by then it will be part of the publisher's catalog that you no doubt receive.

Sometimes it's just plain difficult to decide what to keep and what to safely toss. Below are some questions to ask yourself about the item to determine it's value and importance. Along with these questions, always ask "If I don't keep this piece of paper or document, what is the worst possible thing that could happen?" Then decide if you can live with the consequence.

RETAIN OR REJECT?

ASK YOURSELF:	KEEP	TOSS
Could this item be the future's historical document?	Yes	No
Will a genealogist of the future find this document valuable to our family history?	Yes	No
Does someone other than me have a copy of this document if I should need it again after throwing away my copy?	No	Yes
Is the information on the document outdated (such as a family history writing contest you thought about entering that had a deadline of five years ago)?	No	Yes

Remember, it doesn't matter which filing system you decide upon, as long as it's easy to create, use and maintain. It should allow you to retrieve needed documents within seconds. If a system is not working for you, try another. Once you have found a workable system, stay on top of it. All it takes is a few minutes a day to keep yourself organized, and that will pay off immensely when you are preparing for research trips.

FOUR

Making Your Research Trip Count

T he Boy Scouts say it best: Be prepared. Whether you're traveling across country or across town, whether you will be researching for a few hours or a few days, you need to be prepared for your research trip. Preparation involves more than just gathering your pedigree charts and family group sheets and deciding which clothes to wear. There is much more to consider: Where are you going and where will you stay? Who holds the records you need? What can you expect when you get to the repository? When should you go? How can you make the most of the limited time you have at a repository? Why are you going?

While this last question may seem absurd, let me explain. I need research done in Virginia. I have several options for obtaining the research. I can go to the local Family History Center and see if the records I need are available on microfilm. They're not. If I need only a few records and have enough information on the people to easily get the records, then I can write to the appropriate repository, assuming it handles mail requests. If I decide there are too many records to conveniently request them by mail, my final alternatives are to make the trip and do the research myself or hire someone to get the records for me. My first inclination is to go myself; after all, I love doing research, and I want to do the search myself. But is this the most economical solution? If money were no object, I'd be on the next plane; but it is. In the long run, it will probably be less expensive to hire someone there, someone who no doubt knows the repository better than I. So why should I go? (One reason to go, of course, is to visit the places where your ancestors lived. This may or may not be reason enough for you to be on your way.)

Another interpretation of this question has to do with setting research goals. When you are a new genealogist, the goal is to gather anything and everything on everyone, which is overwhelming when you make a research trip. To expedite your search and use your time efficiently, you should write out the objectives you hope to accomplish when you visit a research repository. As you get your feet wet, your research interests tend to narrow, and this makes it easier to define your research goals. You now focus on certain ancestors and families for one reason or another. You may start hitting the proverbial brick wall in research, which requires more time and patience to break through. Or you may have a research project underway that will lead to publication or some other means of distribution.

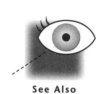

See Also

FOR FURTHER DISCUSSION

See chapter six, starting on page 63, for more on organizing a research project.

RESEARCH JOURNAL

Many genealogists keep a research log, calendar or plan on which they list all the sources they plan to check or have already checked during research trips. I like a research *journal*. Most logs, calendars or planners prompt you to record the date of the search, what you plan to look for or what you found, the source citation and any comments. A research journal goes several steps further: It asks you to record your thought process or your reasoning, your objective and details of variant names you checked.

Like your note-taking and files, keep journal sheets on each surname or family group under study. The journal will keep track of all sorts of records, so there is no need to have a form for each type of record. Also, in the course of research, one record may lead you to another (census to city directories, for example, or vice versa), and you need to be able to record the thought process that led you from one record to another.

On the journal (see the Research Journal form on page 41), you begin by recording what you plan to research—say, the 1880 census. Since you more than likely know in which repository you will check the census, fill in that column. While you do not yet have the complete citation for the census, you do know certain parts: the year, the state and perhaps the county. The next column is your objective, what you are looking for. In this case, you're simply looking to see if Winifred Stuart is on the census.

Next is the reasoning or thought process that leads you from one record to another. Don't ignore this column. I know of several genealogists (myself included) who have made notes to check this or that source, then by the time they make their next research trip, they have totally forgotten *why* they had intended to check it. The source may not be one you would routinely seek, but information in some other record gave you a clue that pointed you in that direction. If you set your research aside for any length of time, you may not remember why you needed to see if there was, say, a divorce.

As you conduct your search, you will fill out the other columns: date, the complete source citation, the name variations you checked and the results of the search. The name variations column is also one to not ignore. Later in your research you may find a totally new way of spelling a name which hadn't occurred to you. Now you can check your journal to see if any searches ended with negative results and recheck those records for this new name variation.

RESEARCH JOURNAL
(before research)

Surname_____Stuart_____   Soundex code_____S363_____

Date	Repository	Source Citation	Objective	Reasoning	Name Variations Checked	Results
	Penrose Library 20 N. Cascade Ave. Colorado Spgs, CO	1880 Census, Colorado, El Paso Co.	To locate Winifred and his family in the census.			

RESEARCH JOURNAL
(after research)

Surname_____Stuart_____   Soundex code_____S363_____

Date	Repository	Source Citation	Objective	Reasoning	Name Variations Checked	Results
20 Aug 1998	Penrose Library 20 N. Cascade Ave. Colorado Spgs., CO	1880 Census, Colorado, El Paso Co., ED 43, p. 21, #159-159	To locate Winifred and his family in the census.			Made photocopy
20 Aug 1998	Penrose Library	Colorado Springs City Directory, 1883, p. 276 (individual listing); p. 175 (ad for his store)	To locate Winifred and his business in the city directory. To see if there are ads for his store.	1880 census showed he owned a dry goods store.	Stuart, Stewart, Steward	Found individual listing under Stewart and an ad for his store. Made photocopies.
20 Aug 1998	Penrose Library	Gazette Telegraph newspaper, obituary index	To see if there is an obituary for Winifred.	Winifred d. 23 Oct. 1888. There should be an obituary.	Stuart, Stewart, Steward	Could not find a listing for him in the index.
	Penrose Library	Gazette Telegraph	Check actual newspaper on the days surrounding his death date.	He may have been missed in the indexing.		

This research journal form is used to plan and keep track of research. **Before:** The first version shows the sort of information you'll note before the research trip: where you're going, what you're likely to research and why you're researching it. **After:** The second version shows the results of your initial research, as well as other research conducted during the trip and the next item to check on a subsequent trip.

Note: The Soundex code refers to a surname indexing system based on the way surnames sound without reliance on exact spellings. A full explanation of the Soundex system itself is beyond the scope of this book.

By leaving the date blank until you have done the search, you can quickly glance down the column and see what you still need to do. This journal will become part of your research notebook, which you will carry with you on all research trips.

RESEARCH NOTEBOOK

Your research notebook can either be a paper version in a binder or a laptop computer version. I use both. In my binder I have the following items:

- research journal
- pedigree charts
- family group sheets, fully documented (If you are filing by couple/family group, you will need to either pull these from your files each time you go on a research trip and refile them upon your return, or you will need to keep duplicate copies in your research binder. If you use duplicates, make sure you keep both copies identical and updated.)

In my laptop, I have the following items accessible should I need them:
- record abstracts from previous research
- notes from previous research trips

A Useful Form You Can Reproduce

For a full-sized blank copy of the Research Journal form, see page 139. You are free to photocopy this form for personal use.

Definitions

FOR FURTHER DISCUSSION

See page 12 in chapter two, for a simplified explanation of the *ahnentafel* numbering system.

Some researchers use genealogical software programs on their laptops containing the data normally printed on pedigree charts and family group sheets. All they need to do is bring up the information on their screens. This eliminates the need to carry all of that paper. This is certainly convenient, but I don't use a genealogical software program for two reasons, one of which I explained in chapter one. The other reason is that I'm a tactile person. Not only do I want to see the chart, but I need to hold it, make notes on it, and carry it around with me, if necessary.

Arrange your charts and group sheets in your research binder according to the numbering system you have chosen, or that was chosen for you if you are using a limited genealogical software program. **Most pedigree charts use the *ahnentafel* numbering system**, so I arrange my charts and family group sheets numerically by this system within my research binder. This arrangement coordinates well if you are using the filing system by couple or family group.

In your notebook, your research journals can be kept in alphabetical order by surname or behind each family group sheet. Use subject dividers labeled "research journals" (if you are grouping them together), "pedigree charts" and "family group sheets."

You may decide to keep other items such as photocopies of maps, handy in your binder. Try to limit items within your binder to the bare necessities. I would recommend using only a standard, three-ring binder not thicker than two inches. The bigger it is, the heavier it will become. You may want to have separate binders if you work on your spouse's genealogy, too. If you are also researching collateral lines and have family group sheets on aunts, uncles and cousins, this will add to the bulk. (This, of course, is the great advantage of using a laptop computer and genealogical software to manage all of your data. You can easily take it all with you.) From your binder, you may want to weed out some of these charts before you depart— those lines you will not be researching on this trip. Let's face it, even if you are spending two weeks in Salt Lake City at the Family History Library, you will not be able to work on every family. This is the reason for thinking about *why* you are making the trip in the first place and establishing research goals, objectives and priorities.

RESEARCHING YOUR TRIP

Now that your binder and/or laptop are ready to go, you have research of a different nature to do before you leave. You need to research the repository you plan to visit. Write or call the library, courthouse or archive and see if they have a brochure that gives the hours, a summary of the research collection, and other relevant data that will make your trip go smoother.

Make checklists for each repository you plan to visit, update them before a trip and place them, along with any brochures, in a file labeled with the name of the repository. Here is the type of information you need:

- the repository's address and directions to get there
- nearest places to park and the cost
- hours of operation, including whether they close for lunch
- special holidays they close for (a founder's day or state holiday, for example)
- special closures or limitations if the building is being renovated or repaired
- the name of a contact person to whom you can talk upon arrival
- cost of photocopies (both for standard photocopy machines and microprinters)
- restrictions on photocopying (e.g., will you be able to make the copies yourself or must a staff member do it?)
- whether a change machine (or a cashier to make change) is available (some microprinters will only take dimes or nickels, for instance)
- handicap access (such as ramps and elevators)
- research restrictions (e.g., some repositories only allow paper and pencil in the research room—no laptops or briefcases. Are there lockers to store these items? What is the cost?)
- off-site record storage and access
- special collections, indexes, finding aids
- nearest places to eat
- local lodging

Even if you receive a brochure with this information, you may find it handier to extract it onto the checklist. You can easily punch the checklist and put it in your research binder before you leave; your binder may not accommodate a brochure so easily.

A Useful Form You Can Reproduce
For a full-sized blank copy of the Research Repository Checklist form, which provides space for logging all the information in this checklist, see page 140. You are free to photocopy this form for personal use.

PLANNING YOUR TRIP

You should consider the time of year you plan to take your trip. Popular research repositories such as the National Archives in Washington, DC, and the Family History Library in Salt Lake City, Utah, are more crowded in the summer months than winter. The Daughters of the American Revolution Library in Washington, DC, is closed to nonmembers for the month of April, when the members have their national conference. If you are visiting a county courthouse, you may want to find out if any state fairs or local events are planned for the time you will be there; these make parking and finding a place to eat and stay more difficult.

Check to see what days are set aside for the town's cemetery cleanup. In small communities, this is often a week or so before Memorial Day and again in the fall. If you can plan a visit for this occasion, it may benefit your research. No doubt some old-timers will participate in the cleanup and may likely know something of the people buried there or living relatives still in the area.

Idea Generator

If you cannot plan a visit for this time, see if someone in the area would be willing to put a contact note at the grave of your ancestor. I'm serious. At her client's request, professional genealogist Marcia Wyett placed a note at the grave of her client's ancestor. It read, "Looking for all descendants of [client's ancestor]. Please contact Marcia at. . . ." She thought using duct tape to stick the note to the gravestone would be rather tacky, so instead she purchased a small potted plant and attached an envelope marked "To the Relatives of [client's ancestor]" with the note inside. On the Friday before Memorial Day weekend, she placed the plant next to the headstone. It worked: A descendant called on Monday evening.

Efficient Genealogy Vacations

Those of us who are hopelessly addicted to genealogy will take advantage of the yearly family vacation to do a little research on the side. Some even go so far as to refuse to go on any vacations (like on a cruise or to Hawaii) where there is no place to do research. If your spouse and children share your interest, this won't pose any problem. Otherwise, you need to plan carefully. Coordinate with your family a day for them to take in some activity where they won't miss your presence, then hightail it to the courthouse or wherever. I did this once. Now I am constantly reminded of it when my husband says, "Remember that day at Universal Studios? Oh, that's right. You weren't there."

You may have to compromise and promise to limit your research to an afternoon or a morning or, if you're lucky, a full day. Sometimes whining helps get you another day. Or you can explain to them how you were in the midst of making this fabulous discovery at closing time (which does happen a lot!) and you really need to go back tomorrow. While this technique will work once or twice, families tend to wise up eventually.

Another method is to put your family members to work for you. Involve them in your research project. Sometimes this is easier said than done, but money can be a great incentive for some family members. Hire teens to retrieve or replace records or rolls of microfilm for you. Depending on their age and interest, you can even hire them to do some simple research. If you have a teenager who has just gotten a learner's permit or driver's license, you won't even need to pay the adolescent to drive you places. You can use the time in the car to go over your notes and research plan. While my family would look at me as though I were from another planet if I suggested they go to a research repository with me and—you've got to be kidding—*help* me research, they do enjoy visiting a cemetery with me. Here they will gladly go row by row and help me search out a gravestone.

EFFICIENT NOTE-TAKING

If you don't have a laptop computer and you are heavily into genealogy, I recommend you get one. **While I still take notes by hand occasionally, a laptop saves me so much time.** When I want to transcribe a document, it's so much quicker and easier to type on my laptop than to hand copy. Once I've made the transcription, I can print a copy for my notes, copy it into a project or report, or make printouts to send to relatives. I can also keep my notes and transcriptions on my hard drive or on a disk for reference when I make other research trips. If you have poor handwriting, your relatives and descendants will thank you for taking notes on a laptop.

If you've become fax and E-mail dependent, having a modem in your laptop will keep you in touch with the world and keep you from experiencing withdrawal while on a research trip. For downtime, you can load or bring along computer games. Some researchers like to listen to music while

Timesaver

Tip

TIPS FOR LAPTOP NOTE-TAKING

As you become accustomed to using a laptop, you will likely find that your note-taking habits improve since, for many, it is less tiring to type than to write longhand. More complete abstracts become the norm, and there may be less hesitation to transcribe a document that is difficult to comprehend. Such transcriptions help avoid later misinterpretation. To those who would argue that a faster method would be to just photocopy a pertinent document, consider that the document obviously needs careful examination before you proceed further. The typing of a transcript or an abstract provides the opportunity to make that in-depth study. And, later on, it is much simpler to review your computer-entered version than to fish the photocopy out of a pile of papers and decipher the document all over again. Plus, the legibility of a document in the original or microfilm version is sometimes better than in a photocopied one.

When working with deed indexes, divide the computer screen into two panes or columns. Keep the index entries in one and your abstracts in the other. After abstracting a deed, toggle back to the index and place an asterisk by the appropriate entry. Place another mark—perhaps a plus sign—if you also photocopied the document.

—Gale Williams Bamman, CG

Adapted from *Association of Professional Genealogists Quarterly* 8 (September 1993): 59-60.

they research or during downtime, using headphones, of course, while in the research facility.

Another benefit to a laptop is the use of a catchy screen saver to attract attention and generate conversation from other researchers. I've seen laptops with screen savers depicting ancestors' photographs or surnames being researched. This is a great way to meet potential genealogy cousins.

On rare occasions, however, I have wanted to throw my laptop against the wall. On one trip to the Family History Library in Salt Lake City, I had spent six hours taking notes onto my laptop from six reels of tax records. I was on the last reel, and I had been routinely saving every few entries. My word processor malfunctioned and refused to let me save any more on that file or as a new one, either to my hard drive or a floppy. No matter what I tried it wouldn't let me save the document. Computers seem to have a mind of their own; mine transformed my file into a temp file, still wouldn't save it, and as a result, I ended up losing the entire file. I still don't understand what went wrong. So then I had to decide whether to redo six hours of work or reconstruct the essentials from memory. I chose to reconstruct—using paper and pen.

Whether you use a laptop or take notes by hand, here are some tips to make note taking easier and more efficient.

Remember that your note-taking should coordinate with your files. The note-taking form on page 19 is designed for the surname/record type filing system. The one at page 18 is designed for the filing system by couple or family group. Both forms prompt you to cite the source in which you are researching, then allow space for your notes or an abstract of the record. You can also adapt either form on your computer, if you prefer taking notes in that manner.

If you are researching at the Family History Library in Salt Lake City or one of its worldwide centers, it is easy to make a printout from the Family History Library Catalog of the source you'll be checking and take notes on the printout. The source is completely cited on the printout, so you will not have to spend time recopying the information. (It is a good idea, however, to double-check the cataloging citation against the actual publication. Catalogers sometimes make mistakes.) At the top of the printout, record the surname you are searching and either highlight the record type or write it on the upper right corner so it is quickly identified. If you are looking for more than one surname or family in this source, then you have a couple choices: Make another printout (which is currently the cost of making a photocopy) or use your note-taking form for the other surname. Though you will use a lot of paper, it is important to use one form or printout per surname or couple to comply with your filing system.

Do not rush when you take notes. Write legibly. I'm sure you have experienced finding a piece of paper with notes you wrote several months or years ago and having trouble reading or deciphering them. Did "N. Castle" mean "North Castle" or "New Castle"? Get in the habit of only using abbreviations if they are part of the original document. That will save you from

Important

wondering if the abbreviation was that way in the original or per your own shorthand.

If you are using a checklist or to-do list rather than a research journal, after you check an item, note the full results. Just writing "No" or "Negative" or "Okay" means nothing to anyone, especially you a few weeks after you write it. You do not want to have to waste your time rechecking a source.

PHOTOCOPYING, ABSTRACTING, TRANSCRIBING

Another method of note-taking is simply making photocopies of documents you find, then recording the source citation directly on the photocopy, or better yet, also copying the source's title page. One may argue that this method can become expensive, which is true, since microfilm printouts are usually twenty to twenty-five cents each. But if your time in a repository is limited, then you have to weigh the cost against the value of your time. Another disadvantage to this method is that often the microfilm appears crystal clear on the screen, but the photocopy is difficult to read. You may still want the photocopy for your records, but it will be easier to read the information later if you transcribe or abstract the record while looking at the microfilmed original on the screen.

To transcribe a document means to copy the record in its entirety, word for word, with exacting accuracy. Making an abstract of a record means you are copying the pertinent parts of the record, leaving out the legal mumbo jumbo. The most commonly abstracted records are wills and deeds. On pages 48 and 49, a transcription of a will, and an abstract of the same will are juxtaposed side by side.

For More Info

FOR FURTHER DISCUSSION

See the bibliography on page 130 for sources on proper abstracting techniques and addresses on page 127 for vendors who sell genealogical forms.

RESEARCH EXPERIENCE EQUALS BETTER TIME MANAGEMENT

It doesn't matter whether you have a week or an hour at a research facility—you will never have enough time, so you must prioritize your research. This is why it is so important to think about your research goals and why you are making the trip in the first place. As you gain experience in genealogical research, you will learn which records are most likely to give you the information you are seeking. For instance, you want to find the passenger arrival list for an ancestor. Ask yourself what information you need to know to find the list. You need information specific to the ancestor (name, year of arrival, age at arrival, country of origin) and information specific to the record (availability and indexes). If you don't have the information you need to get to the document you want, such as the year your ancestor arrived in America, you need to think about other records that could supply you with that information. In other words, which documents will get you to your goal quickest? Perhaps a naturalization record or census enumeration

TRANSCRIPTION OF THE WILL OF JACOB SHOUGH

Patrick Co., Va.
Will Book 8: 113–14
Recorded 7 Feb 1892

I, Jacob Shough of the County of Patrick and State of Virginia, being of sound and disposing mind and memory do make and publish this as my last Will and Testament in manner and form following, that is to say: I hereby revoke all former will or wills by me at any time made heretofore.

First: It is my will and desire that after my death my body be decently buried according to the rites of my church and condition in life.

Second. It is my will and desire that my executor herein after named pay, as soon as may be convenient after my death, all of my just debts.

Third. I will and bequeath to my beloved wife, Lucy F. Shough all of my estate both real and personal of every kind and description whatsoever, to have and to hold during her natural life.

Fourth. It is my will and desire that after the death of my said wife my said property shall be disposed of as follows: I give to my eldest son Richard Watson Shough, one half of my mill on Spoon Creek, together with one half of my household and kitchen furniture, also one half of my cider mill and he is to have my family Bible and my watch, and to my son Henry Bascom Shough I give one half of said mill on Spoon Creek and one half of my cider mill and one half of my household and kitchen furniture, and he is also to have my horse or mule, whichever it may be, one horse wagon, saddle, gear, farming tools, cooking stove and implements therewith and the residue of such stock as may be left after the payment of funeral expenses, if there should not be a sufficient amount of money on hand to pay same, shall be equally divided between my two said sons.

My said son Henry Bascom Shough shall have in fee simple all of my land other than that part of the land attached to my said mill.

My daughter Mary Stuart Gregory is to have after the death of my said wife, my wifes [sic] gold locket, my silver Tea spoons, and clock, one rocking chair, (the one promised her,) and all wearing apparel and such other little notions as my wife may have at the time of her death.

What may be left of my library I desire my children to divide among themselves as they see fit, except Clark's commentaries which I give to my grand daughter, Carrie B. Wonyeath, having given her mother heretofore in various ways an amount now deemed equal to the shares of my other children. I hereby nominate and appoint my said wife my executor of this my last will and testament and desire that no security be required of her when she qualifies. Witness my hand this 4th day of March 1887.

[signed] Jacob Shough
Signed and acknowledged in our presence and in the presence of the testator at his request as and for his last Will and Testament.

Wm. W. Moir
L.A. Rucker

In Patrick County Court, Febry. 7, 1892.
The last Will and Testament of Jacob Shough decd. was presented in court, proven by the oaths of L.A. Rucker and Wm. W. Moir, the subscribing witnesses thereto and ordered to be recorded.

Copy.   Teste

L.A. Rucker, Clerk

ABSTRACT OF THE WILL OF JACOB SHOUGH

Patrick Co., Va.
Will Book 8:113–14
Date Made 4 March 1887
Date Will Presented and Recorded 7 Feb 1892

Testator: **Jacob Shough**

Being of sound and disposing mind and memory

Revokes all former will or wills made at any other time

Desires a decent burial according to rites of his church and his condition in life

Desires executor pay all his debts

Bequeaths:

To wife, Lucy F. Shough, all his estate, real and personal, during her natural life. Upon her death, his property shall be divided as follows:

To eldest son, Richard Waston Shough, ½ of my mill on Spoon Creek, ½ household and kitchen furniture, ½ of my cider mill, family Bible, and my watch.

To son, Henry Bascom Shough, ½ of my mill on Spoon Creek, ½ household and kitchen furniture, ½ of my cider mill, horse or mule, one horse wagon, saddle, gear, farming tools, cooking stove and implements, residue of stock left after payment of funeral expenses. If not sufficient amount to pay him, stock shall be equally divided between two said sons. Henry shall also have in fee simple all land other than that part of land attached to said mill.

To daughter, Mary Stuart Gregory, my wife's gold locket, my silver teaspoons, a clock, the rocking chair promised her, all my wife's wearing apparel, and other little notions my wife may give her.

My library is to be divided among my children as they see fit.

To granddaughter, Carrie B. Wonyeath, Clark's commentaries, "having given her mother heretofore in various ways an amount now deemed equal to the shares of my other children."

Appoints wife executor. Requests she does not pay any security.

Signed Jacob Shough

Witnesses: Wm. W. Moir and L.A. Rucker, Clerk

Sample Will Abstract
In contrast with the transcription, the abstract covers just the pertinent information, almost in bullet form, so it is quick and easy to read. Rather than rereading the document every time, especially if the handwriting is difficult to read in the first place, it is much easier to refer to an abstract and carry it with your research. Vendors who sell genealogical charts and forms also offer abstracting forms, which prompt you to record the pertinent information.

See the Checklist of Abstracting Items on page 50 for a rundown of the types of information you will include in an abstract.

CHECKLIST OF ABSTRACTING ITEMS

WILL/PROBATE

- type of record (will, inventory, intestate proceedings, etc.)

- source citation (book, page[s], file number, microfilm number)

- repository name and address

- name of testator (person making the will)

- personal information ("of sound mind and body," desired burial, etc.)

- names and relationships (if given) of executors

- date the will was signed

- date the will was entered into probate

- signature or mark of testator

- names and addresses (if given) of witnesses

- bequests (names, relationships, items each person is to receive, including land descriptions)

DEED

- type of record (warranty deed, quitclaim deed, gift deed, etc.)

- source citation (book, page[s], file number, microfilm number)

- repository name and address

- name of grantor(s) (seller) and grantee(s) (buyer)

- date of deed

- date deed was recorded

- the consideration (the amount the land was sold for, the item(s) it was traded for, or if it was a gift)

- signatures or marks of all parties

- names of witnesses

- legal description of the property

- release of dower (this is where the wife relinquishes her rights to the property)

- date, place and by whom the deed was acknowledged

- other information (residences, occupations, relationships of all parties)

Timesaver

will do it. **Knowing this comes with experience, and as you gain experience, you will manage your research time better.**

I had asked one of my cousins, who was helping me research our family, to check for some obituaries in the newspapers at her local library. She is a budding genealogist and did not know that library staff or volunteers often create indexes to many old newspapers. I didn't think to tell her to look for an index, so needless to say, she spent more time than she needed to by hunting through newspapers to locate the obituaries. Granted, indexes are not flawless; omissions and errors occur. But it sure is a lot quicker to start with an index if there is one.

DURING THE TRIP

If you are on an extended research trip, say, to the Family History Library in Salt Lake City or to the locality where your ancestors lived, take a morning or afternoon midway during your trip to digest what you have gathered. Most genealogists wait until they are home to start entering new data or rereading the documents they've acquired. At this point they realize they should have checked such and such. By taking a few hours' break during your trip, you may spot these areas in time to do something about it while you're still there.

Don't think you will do this kind of review at the end of the day when you are tired, unless you happen to be a night owl. As your mother warned you when you tried to write your term paper the night before it was due, when you are tired you can't possibly do your best work. Although you are not being graded on this assignment, who wants to leave a sloppy genealogy for the next generation?

Warning

AFTER THE TRIP

When you get home, log the information from your notes onto your family group sheets and pedigree charts (if you didn't during your trip), making sure you cite the sources again on your family group sheets.

Step By Step

Once this is done, retrieve the appropriate folder, log the information on the table of contents if you're using the surname/type of record system, then file it. For example, you have notes on a marriage of a Fitzhugh to a Conway. Pull both the FITZHUGH: Marriage Records and the CONWAY: Marriage Records files. Log the information onto the Fitzhugh table of contents and assign the document the next consecutive page number, then file it. In the Conway file, do the same thing, only in the enclosure/page number column you will cross-reference the Fitzhugh file: "see Fitzhugh, enc. 4." As mentioned in chapter two, you could also make a photocopy of the document and put one in each file; however, this adds to the amount of paper you will accumulate.

Whether you're filing by couple or family group, you'll enter the new information on your family group sheets and cite your sources. But you will file the notes and records according to the footnote number you assigned to the source of information.

If you have used a laptop to make abstracts or transcriptions or to take notes, make printouts as soon as you get home, and back up your computer files. Keep the notes on your laptop, too, since this is an easy way to bring along past research notes for reference.

Make it a rule that you do not allow yourself to make another research trip before you have updated and entered all the data from a previous trip and have filed your notes and documents. This is beneficial not only for your method of organization, but also because you don't want your research to go cold. The longer you wait, the more you will be asking yourself, "Now, why did I copy this?" or "What does this say?" or "What does 'no' mean?" Even your own handwriting can become cryptic. On the next trip, you don't want to duplicate what you have just done, which could happen if you haven't taken clear, thorough notes and updated your data from the last trip. You may also want to follow the rule that you must enter all the data from a trip by a certain deadline, such as within one or two weeks.

Tip

COLOR CODING FAMILY GROUP SHEET DATA

Starting in 1960, I wrote out everything in longhand and ended up with seventeen thousand documented family group sheets with which to write my books. One thing that helped then—and can still help now if there is a need to write something by hand—is to color code all the entries. In other words, I assigned a different color of ink to each specific church book as I noted the entries therein. I remember that Kingston, New York, Reformed Church entries were recorded in a bright green color on my family group sheets; Schoharie, New York, Lutheran Church entries were written in a slate gray, etc. The point of all this was that as I collected more and more entries on my family group sheets, I really didn't have to literally read them as I went along; I could almost subliminally sense what record I was looking at by quickly skimming the colors of the respective notations. This ended up saving lots of time as the project progressed.

—Henry Z Jones Jr., FASG

SOURCE CITATIONS

By now you have surely realized that you will be citing your source of information many times:

- in your research journal
- on your notes, abstracts, transcriptions and photocopies
- on your family group sheets
- on your table of contents page in your files

Important

Citing sources is *not* optional in genealogy. Without getting on a very tall soapbox, I have to say that you will never remember where you got each piece of information, you don't want to repeat the effort, and you may want to return to that source when you uncover new surnames for that area. Remember, too, that genealogy is a legacy. Once again, why are you researching your family history? Though there are many reasons, no doubt one of them is to leave something for your children and grandchildren. Even though you may think that no one cares where the information came from, someday someone will. Do them and yourself a favor and document your sources. It certainly doesn't hurt to do so, and it only takes an extra minute or so of your time. Besides, if you ever decide to publish the results of your research, either as an article or a book, you will need to cite your sources.

For More Info

FOR FURTHER DISCUSSION

For the finer points on proper source citations, consult Elizabeth Shown Mills's *Evidence! Citation and Analysis for the Family Historian* (see the bibliography for details).

CHECKLIST OF THINGS TO DO FOR A RESEARCH TRIP
Before the Trip
- Compile a research notebook.
- Prepare research journals or plans.
- Research the facility and locality where you are visiting.
- Research holidays and observances that may affect your trip.
- Pack research items (notebook, laptop computer, forms, etc.).

During the Trip
- Take thorough, clear notes according to your filing system.
- Make photocopies, abstracts or transcriptions as needed.
- Take a morning or afternoon off at the midpoint of your trip to digest what you have acquired.

After the Trip
- Review all your notes and photocopies.
- Enter new data on your family group sheets and cite sources of information.
- File notes and documents according to your filing system.

Before the Next Trip
- Review your information from the last trip.
- Log in your research journal sources you need to check for the upcoming trip.
- Research the repository you will be visiting (if this is your first time there), then revise and update your journal accordingly.
- Start packing!

Ah, the packing. What should you take besides your research notebook and laptop computer? The next chapter has some answers.

FIVE

Packing for Research Trips

I am not known for packing light. It's all my mother's fault. She drilled into me the axiom "It's better to have it and not need it than to need it and not have it." So I rarely do not have something I need. Of course, I can't go anywhere without two suitcases, my laptop case and my research tote bag. To ensure you'll have everything you need either make lists or keep a stocked briefcase or tote bag for each type of research endeavor.

In genealogy, if you think you can get by with just one briefcase or tote bag, you are mistaken. You will need at least four to be prepared for each unique research trip. Don't panic. You probably won't take all of these on the same trip. The idea is to keep items for specific trips organized and to prevent you from forgetting something. One tote bag is for a typical research trip to record repositories, another is for conducting oral history interviews, a third is for research trips to cemeteries, and a fourth is for attending genealogical society meetings.

Before we get into the contents of each tote bag, let's look at an important part of packing for your trip: what to wear. Now, men, don't think this is only a concern for the ladies. This is relevant to you, too, so don't skip this part.

DRESSING FOR YOUR TRIP

In Simla, the rural community in eastern Colorado where I live, if you are dressed up, you must be going to a funeral. No, I take that back. If you are in your dress jeans and Sunday-best cowboy hat, you must be going to a funeral. American society pretty much goes casual these days. When we dress, we think comfort. When you go on a research trip, you also think comfort, but you can be too casual or too dressy for certain repositories.

Think about where you plan to conduct research and pack accordingly.

SUGGESTED ATTIRE FOR . . .

	Ladies	Gentlemen
Courthouse	blouse with slacks or skirt; dress; business suit (dark colors)	slacks, dress shirt and tie; suit (dark colors)
Cemetery	T-shirt or sweatshirt, jeans, tennis shoes or boots	T-shirt or sweatshirt, jeans, tennis shoes or boots
Family History Library or Center	dress jeans or slacks, blouse	dress jeans or slacks, sport shirt
National Archives or Regional Branch	skirt or slacks, blouse	slacks, dress shirt, tie
Public or Research Library	dress jeans or slacks or skirt, blouse	dress jeans or slacks, sport shirt
University Library (*if you want to blend with the students*)	jeans or shorts, shirt	jeans or shorts, shirt
University Library (*if you want to blend with the faculty*)	slacks or skirt, blouse; dress; business suit	suit; slacks, dress shirt, tie

If you are researching in a cemetery, for example, you will want to wear jeans with boots or tennis shoes; ladies, you will not wear your spike heels to the cemetery, unless of course you plan to help aerate the lawn. When you enter a courthouse—a place of business—you want to dress nicely and blend in with the staff, but wearing a beige suit or a light-colored outfit may be counterproductive. If the clerk sends you to the attic or basement to look at deed books that haven't been off the shelf since 1892, you will likely regret choosing light-colored clothing. In some courthouses, you may be doing a lot of standing, so comfortable shoes are also important.

Also think about the part of the country you are visiting. In downtown urban areas with lots of business offices, people will be more dressy. In a rural community, people tend to dress more casually. Basically, save the Bermuda shorts, black socks and sandals for Disneyland.

TOTE BAG FOR THE TRADITIONAL RESEARCH TRIP TO A RECORD-REPOSITORY

Naturally, you will tailor the following list of items to include in your research tote bag or briefcase to suit your needs. These are the things I keep in my research bag, so when I'm ready to make a trip, all I need to do is add my research notebook (containing research journals, pedigree charts and family group sheets) and take my laptop computer in its carrying case. I also keep in each tote bag a 4″×6″ card listing all the items I normally

Tip

PACKING PERSONAL ITEMS FOR A TRIP

My mother-in-law taught me to keep a packed cosmetic kit. My husband and I maintain a complete second set of shampoo, lotion, combs, brushes, shavers and the rest in a case that we can grab for travel. This has been a help with all the professional conferences we attend. We never waste time packing such items, we do not arrive to find ourselves out of something we need, and we do not have to pay small-bottle prices for something we buy in bulk at home.

——Katherine Scott Sturdevant, historian

Tip

PREPARING TRAVELING FILES

In my several years as a Family History Center director, I noticed that most people began their research by surname hunting. Some people collect massive files with any incidental mention of a particular name. Usually, this exercise is not very productive.

Rather than collecting names, I encourage researchers to collect localities. For instance, in a New England state, files about specific towns can be very useful, and material can be referenced over and over again. The types of material to collect may include

- periodical articles on local history

- articles containing abstracts of town records

- period and contemporary maps

- important addresses, phone numbers and directions for researching on-site in public and private archives and libraries

- lists of microfilm and microfiche that have been searched

- societies and organizations with local resources

- bibliographies of books and articles on genealogy and local history

I like to set up a traveling file with information on localities I regularly research on-site. When I make my own annotated finding aid of the records I have searched (condition, extent, availability, etc.) on my laptop, I put the printout in a file folder for future reference. This practice has saved me lots of time in not having to start from scratch every time I return to a library, town hall, courthouse, etc.

My traveling files vary from a favorite old accordion file (if I am going by car) to a zippered loose-leaf binder with pockets (great for flying). All that matters is that I can put my hands on information quickly and avoid wasting precious research time. Every minute counts, and the best finds usually come right before it's time to leave. It's embarrassing to be thrown kicking and screaming out of a library five minutes after closing time!

—Christina K. Schaefer, CGRS

take with me, so I can run down the checklist and make sure I replace any items I removed at home before I leave.

- **Paper.** Along with note-taking forms, if you're using them, bring a notepad. Even if you plan to use a laptop to take notes, you will still need a notepad to jot down film numbers, records to search and other odds and ends.

- **Pens, pencils and highlighters.** Some repositories will not allow you to use pens, so it is always a good idea to keep a supply of pencils. Mechanical pencils with a #2 lead are particularly convenient since you're not at the mercy of the repository's pencil sharpener. Remember to bring a supply of extra lead! Everyone loves highlighters, the more colors the better. Keep in mind, however, that if you highlight your ancestor's name on a photocopy, it may cause that part to darken over time and be obliterated should you need to make a photocopy of the photocopy. You may want to consider instead underlining the relevant data with a red pencil or pen. The only problem with using a colored pen or pencil is if you photocopy it, you lose the color. *Never* mark on papers, books or historical documents that belong to someone else, of course.

- **A few sheets of colored paper.** If you are using a microfilm reader that projects the image down onto a white surface, placing a sheet of colored paper on the screen helps cut the glare and makes the image easier to read. Some people prefer pastel colors; others use bold, bright colors. Try several colors to determine your preference. If you are using a microfilm machine in which you must look straight ahead at the image, placing a sheet of paper over the screen will only cover the image, which is projected from within the machine, and just make you look silly.

- **Forms.** In particular, you will want a supply of census extraction forms. These are usually available at research repositories that maintain censuses, by mail order from genealogical vendors **(see addresses on page 127)**, or in books such as Emily Anne Croom's *The Unpuzzling Your Past Workbook* **(see bibliography on page 130)**. Though you may be able to purchase these forms at the repository where you're researching, it's more convenient and economical to keep a supply on hand.

For More Info

- **Magnifying glass** to help with fine print.

- **Coins** for the photocopy machines, although most research repositories have a change machine or cashier. It's always a good idea, however, to bring a starting supply of change.

- **Pocket calculator.** I'm math challenged, so I find it easier to use a calculator than figure in my head or on a notepad when I need to calculate someone's birth year based on the age given in a census. I realize, of course, that digging the calculator out of my bag sometimes takes longer than if I did the math my head or on a sheet of paper, but so be it.

- **Stapler.** You may want to staple photocopies you make from one source.

- **Paper clips.** You can use paper clips for documents you don't want to staple.

- **Self-stick removable notes. At the Family History Library in Salt Lake City, where each microfilm reader is situated in a little cubby, I use the self-stick notes to hang on the surrounding "walls" to remind me of**

Research Tip

things to check that may occur to me while I'm researching something else. Repositories generally do not allow you to use any kind of self-stick note to mark a place in a book for photocopying because of the residue the adhesive leaves, but you can use them to stick temporary notes on your photocopies.

- **Maps of the area where your ancestors lived.** In particular, I like to have a map of the state showing the county names and boundaries. This is especially handy if you are not finding your ancestors in a particular county. You can check your map for the names of surrounding counties, and check those places. State maps listing the counties may be found in books such as **Everton's** *The Handy Book for Genealogists* **and Eichholz's** *Ancestry's Red Book* **(see bibliography, page 130).**
- **Tissues or a hanky.** You'll want these if you are working in a dusty archive or courthouse and have allergies. You can also use tissues or a hanky to clean the glass and lens of a microfilm reader.
- **Emery board.** No, this is not in case you break a nail, but you could certainly use it for that. You can use an emery board as an emergency pencil sharpener.
- **Medications.** There's nothing worse than traveling for hours to get to a research repository then getting a headache or stomachache or allergy attack. Take a supply of painkillers, antacids, antihistamines, antidepressants or whatever else you may need.
- **Snacks.** Though you won't be able to eat these in the research repository, carry some to eat in the snack room or outside. Personally, I cannot concentrate if my stomach is growling, nor can the people around me. Frequent breaks help rejuvenate your mental alertness, which you need for research.

TOTE BAG FOR ORAL HISTORY INTERVIEWS

Before making a trip to visit and interview family members, stock a separate tote bag with the following items and leave in the tote bag a 4″×6″ card with a list of them in case you remove items:

- Cassette tape recorder (and a microphone if none is built in).
- AC cord.
- Supply of cassette tapes and labels.
- Extension cord.
- Extra batteries.
- Notepad and pens.
- List of questions, or a book on oral history interviewing that has sample questions.
- Address book to note relatives' names and addresses the person you are interviewing may give you.
- Your research notebook with pedigree charts and family group sheets.
- Wristwatch or pocket watch to make sure you do not overstay your welcome. Most interview sessions should not last longer than an hour

at a stretch. You need to give yourself and the person being interviewed an occasional break.

- Photocopies of any documents you've gathered to show the relative.
- Photographs you need to identify. If you're bringing original photographs with you, make sure they are carefully protected against tears, scratches and bends.
- Magnifying glass, in case the relative will need it to view the photocopies or photographs.
- 35mm camera with focusable lens, or digital camera, to photograph the person you're interviewing and any documents or photographs your relative won't let you take out of the house to copy. My great-aunts wouldn't let the family Bible out of their possession, so I was glad I had brought my camera. As well as taking notes, I also took pictures of the Bible pages.

You may also consider bringing a laptop computer and scanner.

Tape Tips
Label each tape and its storage case with identifying information:
- the person being interviewed
- the date
- the place

After the interview, immediately punch out the cassette tab, making it impossible for someone to accidentally erase the tape or record over it.

Video for Oral History
You may also use a video camera for oral history interviews. Obviously, you can't keep a spare video camera in a tote bag (unless you have an extra few hundred dollars to invest in one for this purpose only). Instead, keep in your tote bag a list of video accessories you will need:
- video camera
- videocassette tapes and labels
- AC adapter
- charged batteries
- extension cord
- notepad and pens
- list of questions or a book on oral history interviewing that has sample questions
- research notebook
- address book
- wristwatch or pocket watch
- photocopies of any documents you've gathered to show the relative or photographs you need to identify
- magnifying glass
- 35mm camera or digital camera or a laptop computer and scanner

A discussion of how to organize and store oral history tapes begins on page 84 in chapter seven; for now let's concentrate on the paper that an interview generates. Whether you are taking notes at the time of the interview or not, at some point you will either want to transcribe the tape or make notes from it. Use a similar format for your notes or transcription as you have for your other research: surname in the upper left; "oral history interview" in the upper right; source citation (e.g., "Interview with Jeremy Helms, 416 Pueblo Ave., Colorado Springs, CO, by Sharon DeBartolo Carmack, 5 February 1996"). If you are filing by couple or family group, file the interview under the appropriate family.

Once again, you may have the problem of multiple surnames and information in an interview. I choose to file the notes or transcription from the interview under the surname of the person being interviewed (HELMS: Oral History Interview), or in the case of a married woman where your interview deals with her maiden name and family, I file it under her maiden name. Thus, "Interview with Mary (Fitzhugh) DeBartolo," would get filed as FITZHUGH: Oral History Interview. If the interview also dealt with her husband's family, cross-reference the interview in the husband's surname file's table of contents.

Tip

TOTE BAG FOR A TRIP TO THE CEMETERY

After a research repository, the cemetery is a genealogist's favorite place to be. Most make a day of it, bringing along a picnic lunch. Try to pick a brightly colored tote for your cemetery items. This way, if you set down your tote bag in the cemetery and walk away from it, you will be able to spot it easily. Select a waterproof tote bag to protect its contents if the ground is wet or snowy. Stock your cemetery tote bag with the following items:

- Notepad, pens and pencils.
- Research notebook with pedigree charts and family group sheets.
- Carpenter's apron. Because of the many pockets, I find a carpenter's apron handy to carry items such as pens, pencils, notepaper, etc., as I move from tombstone to tombstone.
- Gardener's kneepads. These will help cushion your knees when you have to kneel in front of a tombstone to read it better or to cut away overgrown grass.
- Garden shears to cut away overgrown grass.
- Whisk broom to remove cut grass or dirt from the base of the stone.
- Sunscreen.
- Bug repellent.
- Wet wipes. This is a dirty job, and you will want to wash up for lunch.
- Camera and film.
- Sprayer with water. Sometimes just wetting the stone will help make the image stand out for photographing.
- White chalk.

- Lunch, including something chocolate. Even if you don't take any food, you might want to take water or some other beverage.

Remember, gravestones are historical artifacts. Do not do anything to the stone that may harm it. Never try to clean the stone with a wire-bristled brush or any acid-based products (e.g., vinegar and water) that can eat away the stone. If you use chalk to bring out the image, only use white chalk; colored chalk may stain the stone. Use water in your spray bottle to wash away the chalk residue when you are finished making photographs.

As you record the inscriptions from your ancestors' tombstones, remember that this is an exception to the surname/record type or couple/family group filing rule. You want to preserve the order of the tombstones since relatives with different surnames are often buried in close proximity. Either place photocopies of your notes in the appropriate files or cross-reference them.

TOTE BAGS FOR GENEALOGICAL SOCIETY MEETING

Most genealogists belong to at least one genealogical society, usually a local one. Meetings typically feature a speaker, who will distribute handouts to accompany the lecture. Here is another area where preference will determine how you file the handouts when you get home. You can start a binder or a folder specifically for the handouts given at society lectures, or you can create folders for topics—German Research, Pennsylvania Research, Immigration Research—and file handouts in the appropriate file folders. I would not file them by speaker's name unless you can easily remember speakers' names and what they spoke about.

As a member, you may want to have a special tote bag to use when you go to society meetings. This will be convenient for bringing home handouts—and extra cookies from break time. Keep in the tote bag your society's membership directory and a pen or pencil so you'll have these items with you at every meeting. Often during meetings, address and phone number changes are announced. If you have your directory with you, you can jot these details down immediately and only once.

It seems when local societies get new members, they become vampirish. Ah, new blood! Before you know it, you are being flattered, cajoled, persuaded, convinced, coaxed, urged and sweet-talked into helping on a committee, taking charge of a committee or becoming an officer. When you make the transformation from innocent member to officer or committee person, you suddenly inherit a file folder, box or storage bin of paper. In chapter six, we'll look at organizing your inheritance (the project), but for now you will need your society tote bag in which to carry pertinent papers to meetings. If your inheritance is small—like a few file folders—keep everything in the tote where you can always find it and where it will be when you leave for the meeting.

Of course, the more active you are in different organizations, the more

Warning

See Also

FOR FURTHER DISCUSSION

See chapter six, page 63, for details on organizing a cemetery transcription project.

tote bags you will need. This should not be a problem, however, because genealogical vendors (through the mail and at conferences) would be pleased to sell you a variety of tote bags with various genealogical illustrations and pithy quotes on them. At some national conferences, you will receive a nice canvas tote bag as part of your registration. (Be careful when you wash them; they will shrink!) Now that I think of it, I think I've purchased only one or two tote bags in my genealogical life, and I must have two dozen of them; the majority I acquired as part of conference attendance.

Be discriminating about the tote bag you use for each organization. If you are active in an organization that sells a tote bag with its logo on it, buy it and use it for your files for that organization. This will help you remember which items go in which tote bag. If your closet space allows it, hang your tote bags emblem side forward on separate hooks.

HEADING HOME

Have you noticed that genealogists have a lot of stuff? And these are just the items they cart around with them. There's a whole lot more to organize and deal with than research-trip paraphernalia. You may also be wondering what to do with all that stuff you are slowly accumulating in your home from this interest. Read on. After we look at organizing some specific projects, I'll discuss organization in your home.

SIX

Organizing a Research Project

A t what point did researching your ancestry turn into a project? When you started, your goal was to collect anything and everything on all of your ancestors. But one day, someone said, "Hey, why don't you do a book?" or, "That would make a great article." Or you said, "I won't rest until I find out Great-Great-Grandma's maiden name and parents," or, "I'm going to start collecting information on all of the Kincaids and publish a newsletter." All of a sudden, your genealogy is a research project.

In addition to your own personal research projects, you may be put in charge of a genealogical society committee project, such as transcribing records or tombstone inscriptions. Or, as an individual wanting to make a contribution to the field of genealogy, you may adopt one of these projects yourself. The focus here is not on organizing and managing a project committee; it is on the project itself.

ESTABLISHING WHERE YOU'RE GOING

Regardless of how you got involved in a project, you quickly discover that you are gathering even more paper and more information that must be handled and processed. For any project, it is important to define your goals and limitations:

- Why are you undertaking the project (to make a contribution to the field, to leave a legacy for your family, temporary insanity, moment of weakness, boredom, etc.)?
- What do you plan to do with the results (publish a book, computerize and distribute, turn over to someone else to publish or distribute, etc.)?
- Have you written out explicit instructions so that if you die someone can complete your project or at least understand what you were trying to do?

- What will be the scope of the project, i.e., what will be included and what will not? (For example, in tracing all the descendants of a couple, will you include adoptive children and stepchildren? In a book project tracing your ancestry, will you include pre-American ancestors, or is that best left for a second volume? If you are transcribing wills, what time span will you cover?)

Certainly, your goals can change and evolve as you work on the project. You may decide that your cutoff date for transcribing land records was too ambitious. Or you may uncover information that takes your research in a whole different direction. Regardless, begin the project by writing out a clearly defined goal (or as English teachers like to say, a thesis statement). Here are a few examples:

Tip

USING A PORTABLE FILE BOX

I have a main filing cabinet for everything but a separate portable file box for the line I am currently working on. That way I can sit in the TV room or kitchen or in the middle of the bed and work. I'm not much of a stay-in-one-place worker.

—Sharon Swint

This study features the Vallarelli family as illustrative of the typical southern Italian/Italian-American experience. It spans four generations: two in Italy during the nineteenth century and two in America during the first half of the twentieth century. This sociohistorical and genealogical account not only documents the Vallarelli family, but also demonstrates the typical, everyday lifestyles and experiences of a South Italian peasant family.

The goal of this project is to transcribe all the tombstones in St. Mary's Cemetery, recording not only the inscriptions, but also the artwork and composition of the stones.

This study will document the lives of the first one hundred landholders in Elbert County, Colorado. Short biographical summaries on each individual will be presented, as well as genealogical data discovered during the research.

The goal of this project is to abstract the wills recorded in Clark County, Nevada, for a fifty-year span, starting from the county's creation in 1909.

Though writing out your goal may seem trivial for some projects, like the will abstracting project above, it serves two purposes: It keeps your project well defined, and it allows someone else to take over the project if need be.

TAILORING YOUR WORK TO YOUR GOAL

Let's look at some of the more common projects genealogists undertake and some ways of organizing your materials to keep you working efficiently and make your job easier when it's time to present the material.

One-Surname Project

Although I'm not big on genealogy software programs, I don't see how anyone could undertake a single-surname project and not use a computer program to sort and link individuals into family groups. One of my future projects (although it may have to be in my next lifetime since this one is already full) is to extract all the DeBartolos from the civil vital records office in Terlizzi, Bari, Italy, to see how they are all related, if they are. For this, I would definitely use a laptop computer and a genealogical software program, which will link children to parents.

Before you begin a project of this or a similar nature, you need to be happy with the software you have selected or make sure the data will transfer completely uncorrupted to a new program should you decide to change.

Another time-saver and organizing tool would be a computer program like **Clooz (see chapter two, page 20) or Sky Filer (see addresses, page 127)**, which allows you to file documents electronically. Even though you may be using an electronic filing program, you will still have paper copies to deal with. This makes the surname/record type filing system all the more usable. You will have only one surname; to have any sense of organization at all, you almost have to file by the type of record. Using this paper filing method in conjunction with an electronic one will free you from hunting for days for a record.

See Also

A single-surname project is one where you absolutely need clearly defined goals. Will you be gathering anything and everything you can find on anyone with this surname, or will you only gather everything on the Zettlemeyers in Ohio?

Are you going to publish a quarterly newsletter? If so, you will have many decisions to make about its contents and its distribution (see discussion about newsletters on page 73). **Consult Betty Summers's article "Business Management for a Family Newsletter"** in the *Association of Professional Genealogists Quarterly* 10 (December 1995): 109-11.

For More Info

Will you be starting a family association? Christine Rose writes for the Federation of Genealogical Societies' *FORUM*, a quarterly column on family associations, in which she notifies readers of newly formed associations and their projects and discusses getting a family association started.

Like all your research projects, a one-surname study has to be flawlessly documented. You will be sharing with others the results of your research or information that is contributed to you. Others will want to know the source of the data. You will be doing no one any favors if you just input names into your computer and do not include the sources of the information.

Beyond the Family Group Sheet

Before discussing organizational methods for other types of projects you may undertake, let's look at what to do with information that doesn't fit conveniently on a family group sheet. We all start out using family group sheets, but many genealogists outgrow them quickly. For example, what do

GENEALOGICAL OR FAMILY SUMMARY

Catlett Conway[6] Fitzhugh (*Mary[5] Stuart, David[4], William Gibbons[3], John[2], Rev. David[1]*) was born 25 April 1831 in King George County;[1] died 22 May 1908 in Greene County, Virginia, and was buried in the Old Fork Episcopal Church Cemetery, Ashland, Hanover County, Virginia.[2]

Catlett married Ellen Stuart Conway, the daughter of Battaile Fitzhugh Taliaferro Conway and Mary Ann Wallace, on 27 November 1860 in Madison County, Virginia. Ellen was born 31 August 1837 in Madison County, Virginia;[3] died 6 March 1912, Louisa County, Virginia, and was buried in the Old Fork Episcopal Church cemetery.[4]

In 1850, nineteen-year-old Catlett was living in Richmond, Virginia, in a household with John H.F. Mayo. At this time, Catlett was working in the woolen business.[5] Ten years later, Catlett was still living in Richmond and working as a merchant.[6] After he married late in 1860, Catlett took up farming in Greene County, Virginia. He did not own land at the time of the 1870 census, but his personal property was valued at $555.[7] In 1880 and 1900, Catlett continued to work as a farmer.[8] [Did he own land then? Check Greene Co. and Hanover Co.]

On 9 September 1860, Thomas A. Marshall sold to his brother-in-law C.C. Fitzhugh two Negro girls, Cordelia and Nolia, "in trust to secure a debt due to Mrs. Mary F. Fitzhugh" of $1,520 by bond.[9] [check 1860 slave schedule] [Did Catlett serve in Civil War? Why were Catlett and Ellen in Alabama in May 1865?]

By 1910, when Ellen was a widow, she had moved to Louisa County. Five of her children were still unmarried and living at home: Conway B. (44), Mary S. (40), Linda T. (35), Jennie S. (32), and Stuart D. (27).[10] [Check Greene Co., Va., for will of Catlett in 1908; check Louisa Co., Va., for will of Ellen in 1912.

Children:[11]

 i Child, d. by 1870.[12]

---

[1] Madison Co., Va., Marriage Register 1:12, FHL 32595; tombstone inscription, Old Fork Episcopal Church, Ashland, Hanover Co., Va.
[2] Obituary, *The Daily Progress* [Charlottesville, Va.], 27 May 1908; tombstone inscription, Old Fork Episcopal Church, Ashland, Hanover Co., Va.
[3] Madison Co., Va., Marriage Register 1:12, FHL 32595.
[4] Madison Co., Va., Marriage Register 1:12, FHL 32595; tombstone inscription, Old Fork Episcopal Church, Ashland, Hanover Co., Va.
[5] 1850 Census, Virginia, Henrico Co., Richmond, p. 256, #340-397.
[6] 1860 Census, Virginia, Henrico Co., Richmond, 2d Ward, p. 121, #611-761.
[7] 1870 Census, Virginia, Greene Co. Standardsville, p. 75, #519-519. The General Index to Deeds for Greene County was checked, 1835-1912, FHL 31715, there were no listings for Catlett.
[8] 1880 Census, Virginia, Greene Co., Standardsville, ED 59, p. 9, #80-80; 1900 Census, Virginia, Hanover Co., Beaver Dam Dist., ED 20, sheet 21B #405-414.
[9] Orange Co., Va., Deeds 45:329, FHL 33030.
[10] 1910 Census, Virginia, Louisa Co., Louisa Twp., ED 82, sheet 2A, #28-29.
[11] 1870 Census, Virginia, Greene Co., Standardsville, p. 75, #519-519; 1880 Census, Virginia, Greene Co., Standardsville, ED 59, p. 9, #80-80; 1900 Census, Virginia, Hanover Co., Beaver Dam Dist., ED 20, sheet 21B, #405-414.
[12] The 1900 census states that Ellen was the mother of nine children with eight living; in 1910, however, it states Ellen was the mother of eight children with seven living. According to an undocumented genealogical compilation by Mary Stuart Fitzhugh, daughter of John Stuart Fitzhugh, sent to the compiler by Mary Eleanor Fitzhugh Hitselberger of Fond du Lac, WI, a

Vital statistics written in sentences

Chronological discussion of research findings

Notes to remind yourself of research needing to be done

Children of the couple

Analysis of research data

ii HENRY NEWMAN FITZHUGH, b. 20/29 July 1863, Madison Co., Va.; d. 6/14 July 1906.[13]

iii BATTAILE CONWAY FITZHUGH, b. 9 May 1865, Eufaula, Ala.; d. 15 Oct. 1918.[14]

iv MARY STUART FITZHUGH, b. 27 Aug. 1867, Va.; d. 2 March 1952.[15]

v SIDNEY WALLACE FITZHUGH, b. 2 Apr. 1870, Standardsville, Greene Co., Va.;[16] d. 29 Oct. 1926, Green Springs, Louisa Co., Va.[17]

vi VERLINDA TALIAFERRO FITZHUGH, b. 20 Dec. 1871, Va.; d. 22 Aug. 1940.[18]

vii JENNIE SOMERVILLE FITZHUGH, b. 27 May 1875 Va.; d. 6 Sept. 1942.[19]

viii CATLETT CONWAY FITZHUGH, b. 20 June 1878, Va.; d. 24 Sept. 1942.[20]

ix DAVID STUART FITZHUGH, b. 15 June 1881, Greene Co., Va.[21]; d. 28 Sept. 1949.[22]

---

child Drury was born about 1861 and died in infancy. *Descendants of David Stuart of Virginia* compiled by Carol A. Hauk, Huntington, Ind., 1997, undocumented, 30-31, however, states there was a child named Conway b. 15 June 1862, d. 8 July 1862. The eldest child named in 1870 is Henry Newman, so this ninth child was born and died probably between the time Catlett and Ellen married in 1860 and when Henry was born in 1863.

[13] Genealogical compilation by Mary Stuart Fitzhugh, p. 35, daughter of John Stuart Fitzhugh, undocumented, sent to the compiler by Mary Eleanor Fitzhugh Hitselberger of Fond du Lac, WI.

[14] Tombstone inscription, Old Fork Episcopal Church, Ashland, Hanover Co., Va.; 1870 Census, Virginia, Greene Co., Standardsville, p. 75, #519-519, and 1910 Census, Virginia, Louisa Co., Louisa Twp., Ed 82, sheet 2A, #28-29, both give place of birth as Alabama.

[15] Tombstone inscription, Old Fork Episcopal Church, Ashland, Hanover Co., Va.; obituary, *Richmond Times Dispatch*, 3 March 1952, p. 18.

[16] Greene Co., Va., Birth records, 1853-1919, p. 81, FHL 1976177.

[17] Death certificate, State Department of Health, Vital Records Office, Richmond, Va.

[18] Tombstone inscription, Old Fork Episcopal Church, Ashland, Hanover Co., Va.

[19] Tombstone inscription, Old Fork Episcopal Church, Ashland, Hanover Co., Va.

[20] Tombstone inscription, Old Fork Episcopal Church, Ashland, Hanover Co., Va.

[21] Greene Co., Va., Birth Records, 1853-1919, p. 117, FHL 1976177; tombstone inscription, Maplewood Cemetery, Gordonsville, Orange Co., Va; obituary, *Richmond Times Dispatch*, 29 September 1949, p. 9.

[22] Tombstone inscription, Maplewood Cemetery, Gordonsville, Orange Co., Va.; obituary, *Richmond Times Dispatch*, 29 September 1949, p.9.

---

you do with information you glean from deeds or military records or passenger arrival lists and naturalization records? There just isn't room for this type of information on a family group sheet.

The family group sheet has no place to put your analysis or detailed information about sources. Suppose, for example, you have deduced that an ancestor died between 5 February 1886 and 29 June 1886. You know this because the ancestor made his will on 5 February 1886 and the will was entered into probate on 29 June 1886. There is barely enough room to write the "between" dates, let alone how you arrived at those dates. Or suppose you have discovered two John T. Lawrences living in the same community at the same time. You have analyzed records for both men and concluded that the John T. Lawrence who died in 1750 could not be your John T. Lawrence. Where do you put your analysis and conclusion? You

FILING ACCORDING TO WHERE YOU GO

I keep file folders labeled with the names of repositories I visit. When a miscellaneous question comes up, I note the subject in the folder to wait for the next trip. Sometimes the folders are chock-full of stuff, and other times they are empty. I have several hanging files: for upcoming conferences, for ongoing projects, for pending projects and for correspondence. I especially like the hanging file crates (two stacked on top of one another) on wheels for current work.

——Joy Reisinger, CG

Step By Step

can't on a family group sheet. Family group sheets, like pedigree charts, are meant to record the vital statistics on a family, not much more.

When you have reached the point in your research where you have gone beyond the names, dates and places, where you are doing in-depth research and analysis and gathering historical context, you will need a better way of organizing your data, and I'm afraid you won't find it in a chart or form. Genealogists find writing out the information in narrative form to be the best method. These are called genealogical or family summaries, and you will see them used a lot in the major genealogical journals, such as the *National Genealogical Society Quarterly* or *The American Genealogist*. This format is also widely used if you decide to publish your family history, but it can be equally beneficial to your research to write out all your data as a genealogical or family summary and use a working copy as you would a family group sheet.

The format for a narrative genealogical summary is vital statistics on an ancestor and spouse written in sentence form, followed by a discussion of documented events in their lives, usually presented chronologically. Included in this discussion is analysis of records and research. Sometimes, however, this analysis is part of the footnote instead of in the main text, as in the example shown on page 66. The body of the narrative is followed by a listing of the couple's children.

Even though this example is short, you can see how much more freedom you have to discuss *all* of the information you find. You can also include boldfaced notes in the text reminding you of further research you need to do. Some of the genealogical software programs are now allowing you to write genealogy in a narrative form like this rather than just make pretty charts and forms out of your data.

Although this example does not display a complete numbering system, genealogical summaries typically are written using the Register System or the NGSQ System. See chapter nine for more information on appropriate numbering systems.

Research With the Goal of Writing an Article

Basing an article on your research is a good way to get your family data into print, assuring that it will be around long after you are gone. Articles in genealogical journals generally focus on one to three generations of a family. But once again, what is *your* goal? What is the purpose of writing the article? Most articles have a theme or thesis statement: "to prove that Sarah is the daughter of Isiah and Hannah Weston" or "to separate the two William Gibbons Stuarts living contemporaneously in the same county." This thesis statement is usually found in the first or second paragraph of the article. Although you see this in many articles, please do not write "This paper will prove . . ." or "This paper will show . . ." or "This paper will document. . . ." Wording like this sounds elementary and unsophisticated.

Create a temporary file folder for the records you will gather pertinent to the article. Label this folder with the working title of your article. Pull documents from your permanent filing system and put them in the temporary folder. Even though your documents are all numbered according to your filing system, write on a self-stick removable note the page number you withdrew and adhere the note where that document was filed in your permanent system. Extend the edge of the note slightly so it serves as a tab but will still fit in your file crate or drawer. When the project is over, you can easily refile your documents.

Before you begin writing, think about which journal or magazine you will submit your article to. Each periodical has its own focus and audience, and almost all of them will send you their writer's guidelines if you submit a self-addressed, stamped envelope. Also study recent back issues to get a feel for scope and styles of writing in different articles.

Begin writing the article as soon as you conceive the idea and determine the preferred periodical for your work. There is no better way to see holes than when you start explaining your research in written form. Write your research data into genealogical summaries as discussed earlier. This will also help keep your research goals focused and your "to-do" list up to date.

Keep a separate to-do list specifically for this project, even though it may encompass several surnames. You may also want to have a temporary research binder, keeping in it only those family group sheets and other data relevant to your article.

Allow time for peer evaluations of your article after you are happy with the draft. This is a good way to see if you overlooked any holes in your research and to make sure your writing is clear and understandable to others. Writers are too close to their own material; an outsider will pick up on items that you may have thought were perfectly clear.

Once the article is published, you can refile the documents from your temporary file back into your permanent files, and you can dismantle your temporary binder, placing those items back in your original research binder. I wouldn't do this before publication, because the editor may need clarification or ask you to do additional research.

Always keep a backup copy, in paper and electronic form, of the article you have mailed. Back up the article on a disk and keep it in the file folder you labeled with the article's title. This is now going to be a permanent folder and will hold the copy of the article and any correspondence you have with the journal editor regarding the article. Erase the working title and put the actual title of the published article.

When the article is published, make a photocopy of it—or if you get several copies of the journal as compensation, tear out the pages of your article—and file the article with your draft and the correspondence. If you ever decide to work toward certification, the Board for Certification of Genealogists may want you to submit a copy of the published version, as well as the unedited version you initially sent the journal. Having both together will save time when you gather your materials.

Research With the Goal of Writing a Book

I cannot stress enough the importance of first defining the scope of your book. This will be your guide in organizing your research efforts. Is your goal to compile a bare-bones genealogy, or do you want to produce a compiled genealogy that will explain your research and correct previous errors? Will it cover all the descendants of a couple, or will it cover several surnames, each beginning with the earliest American ancestor?

Most genealogy/family history books are self-published, but you must consider your audience. Typically, it's family members, but don't forget that other genealogists and historians will likely use your work as a reference or as a springboard for their own research. This is why it is so important to document your sources. Sure, your relatives may not care where you got your information, but your colleagues do. Use only standard numbering systems and source citations as I've been discussing throughout this book.

Using the same principles as writing an article, begin writing the book as soon as you decide to write one. Format your research data into genealogical or family summaries. As you write, create a research list to fill the holes you will surely see as you begin drafting the book.

You may want to create checklists of sources to make sure you have researched all possible documents for a family. For example, see page 71 for a census checklist. You can make this kind of checklist for any record group. Make a list of everyone you are covering in your book that may have left a will. For this checklist, record the person's name and the date and place of death. If you have several immigrants at the turn of the twentieth century, make a list of them, the years or approximate years of immigration, and their ages at immigration. These lists will make checking indexes much easier. **(Also see Emily Anne Croom's *The Unpuzzling Your Past Workbook* for various research forms, such as deed and marriage index forms.)**

For writing a book, I think the best filing method is by couple or family group, since this is probably how you will present the material in your book. If you are using the surname/record type filing system, do not create temporary files or pull documents from your permanent files until you are ready to write about a particular family. As you write about a family, pull the documents and have them readily accessible. Then refile them after your project is finished.

I would, however, create a temporary research binder and put in it the family group sheets or genealogical summaries of the generations you will be covering in the book. Create a second binder to hold the current draft of your book. Use divider tabs to separate chapters or generations. After you make corrections to a draft and have entered those changes into the computer, toss the old draft (unless you think you will become a James Michener or a Stephen King, in which case your first draft will be worth millions one day). Always date each draft, especially if you plan to keep old copies. Don't create a new computer file for each revision; you want only one copy that you back up onto a disk at the end of each writing session.

Continue to write as you are researching, entering new data as soon after

A Useful Form You Can Reproduce
For a full-sized blank copy of the Census Checklist, see page 141. You are free to photocopy this form for personal use.

For More Info

CENSUS CHECKLIST

> **Check the column after the couple has been located for that census year**

> **Census to be released to the public in 2002**

> **Although most of this census has been lost, you may find an ancestor in the extant portion or in the 1890 veteran's schedules.**

Name	1790	1800	1810	1820	1830	1840	1850	1860	1870	1880	1890	1900	1910	1920	1930
David & Charlotte Stuart, m. 1806			x	x											
James & Mary Fitzhugh, m. 1830						x	x	x	x						
William Gibbons & Sarah Stuart, M. 1833						x	x	x	x						
Jacob & Lucy Shough, m. 1842							x	x	x	x					
Catlett Conway & Ellen Fitzhugh, m. 1860									x	x					
Arch. & Estell Marshall, m. 1855															
John S. & Susan Fitzhugh, m. 1875															
Francis C. & Margaret (m. 1869) & Louise Fitzhugh (m. 1884)															
Thos. & Louisa Fitzhugh, m. 1857															
Oscar S. & Frances/Louisa Fitzhugh, m. 1855															

On the form, list all the couples you want to locate on census records. As you find them on a particular census, place an X or check mark in that column. I include in the "Name" column the date the couple married, so that I can quickly see on which census they will first appear together. For example, Jacob and Lucy Shough married in 1842, so the first census they will appear on as a couple will be 1850. On earlier censuses, they will be listed with their parents. You can also include death dates so you know when to stop looking for them on the census.

a research trip as possible. Then file the documents according to the system you are using for this project. A large project like this can easily get out of control, so do your best to stay on top of your organizational method.

In the course of writing and publishing a book, you will create several files pertaining to your project:

- photographs and illustrations (masters of those you want to include in the book)
- permissions (if you are going to reproduce material from someone else's work)
- publisher's information (instructions for making camera-ready copy, several price quotes, etc.)
- copyright information (forms and fees to submit to the Library of Congress's Copyright Office)
- ISBN (International Standard Book Numbering) information (so your book can be tracked electronically by booksellers)

- marketing materials (prepublication notices, lists of repositories to whom you will donate copies)
- reviews of your book
- revisions and updates for the next edition

No doubt you will have a projected completion and publication date. Plan now to break it. Very few writers who self-publish a genealogy stay on schedule. Always tack on a couple extra weeks for each stage of your project:

- Writing—creating a draft from your research. How long this takes depends on the amount of material you have gathered and how prolific a writer you are.
- Reviewing and revising drafts. After you have written the entire manuscript, read it in its entirety and make revisions.
- Sending a near-final draft to readers for comments. Always get at least two people, one of whom is familiar with the family, to read the draft for clarity and content. Depending on the length of the manuscript and the reader's schedule, you should allow a reader at least two to three weeks.
- Editing. It's a known fact: You cannot edit or proofread your own work and do it justice. You can try, but you will miss things. Engage a professional editor or someone with editing skills to read your manuscript. Again, the time frame depends on the manuscript length and the editor's schedule.
- Proofreading. Have a different person proofread the camera-ready copy to catch any typos. The time required is probably two to three weeks.
- Indexing. Assuming you are creating the index yourself (see discussion later in this chapter), you need to think about the time to mark the camera-ready copy, enter the data into an indexing computer program, edit the index and proofread it against the text. The time involved depends on the length of your book and your experience as an indexer.
- Publishing. If you have a deadline for having the book ready—a family reunion, for example—find out when the publisher needs the camera-ready copy. The publishing and binding process generally takes a couple of months.

Cemetery Transcription Projects

Compiling and publishing a book of tombstone inscriptions is one of the most fun projects genealogists undertake. If you haven't done a project like this, seriously consider it. It is a great way to make a contribution to the field of genealogy. Because many people cannot visit a distant cemetery themselves, they hope that someone has transcribed the graveyard and published the results. In 1993, I took on a cemetery transcribing project to record tombstone inscriptions from five eastern Colorado cemeteries. During the summer of that year, I spent several hours a day in the cemetery. And what a peaceful place to work! Because I am not a morning person, I

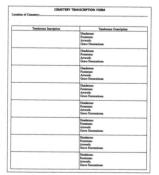

A Useful Form You Can Reproduce

For a full-sized blank copy of the Cemetery Transcription Form, see page 142. You are free to photocopy this form for personal use.

usually visited the cemetery around dusk. Sunsets are stunning from a cemetery, since most graveyards are located on hilltops.

My goal was to record not only the tombstone inscriptions, but also the composition of each marker (granite, marble, wood, metal), the artwork carved on the tombstone (doves, lambs, flowers, horses, cattle brands) and decorations on each grave (artificial flowers, rocks, toys). For this project I used a cemetery transcription form I designed (see the Cemetery Transcription Form on page 74). Taking a clipboard stocked with a bunch of the forms, I went row by row and recorded information about each stone, working for a few hours each day. The rest of the day, or on rainy days, I entered the material in the same format as my form into my computer at home. My final copy was simply a computer-generated version of my handwritten notes.

Do not, under any circumstance, arrange the tombstone inscriptions in alphabetical order! That is what an index is for. Arranging them in alphabetical order will obscure the discovery of possible relatives buried nearby and make your work less useful to other researchers.

Shortly before you are ready to publish, take a friend and a copy of your printout back to the cemetery and proofread against the tombstones. You will be surprised at how many errors you made.

My project was to be a self-published one (as most cemetery transcriptions are), with a very small print run: one hundred copies. After the final draft was finished, I took the master to a quick-print shop, which made the copies and bound them into softcover 8½″ × 11″ "books." Most were donated to libraries; the rest I sold to locals who had relatives buried in one of the cemeteries.

I have toyed with bringing my laptop to the cemetery should I undertake another project like this. Of course, that would be ideal, since I would only have to copy the information once, and it would eliminate the risk of introducing errors with each additional recording. But I just don't see how I could hold the laptop and type, or find a place to put it as I move from grave to grave. In this situation, the good old standby of pen and paper seems to be the best method.

Family or Genealogical Society Newsletter Organization

If you thought you had your hands full with your own research, wait until you decide to produce a newsletter every quarter or every other month. It's a lot of work, and it never goes away. The cycle keeps repeating itself. It is rewarding, of course, and you will meet and work with a variety of people.

Whether you are taking over the editorship or you are starting a newsletter from scratch, create a file folder for each issue for the upcoming year: March 1999, Vol. 2, No. 1; June 1999, Vol. 2, No. 2; September 1999, Vol. 2, No. 3; and December 1999, Vol. 2, No. 4, for example. If it is a particularly thick newsletter, you may want to use accordion file folders or file jackets (folders that are sealed on three sides). Put everything that pertains

CEMETERY TRANSCRIPTION FORM

Location of Cemetery: _Ramah Public Cemetery, Ramah, El Paso Co., Colorado, on south side of Highway 24._

Section 1, Row 1, from north to south

Tombstone Inscription	Tombstone Description
MITCHELL Carl Lillie 1875-1950 1877-1922	Headstone: _polished red granite_ Footstone: _none_ Artwork: _flowers_ Grave Decorations: _none_
Baby Ronald K. MITCHELL Born Died Nov. 3 Nov. 13 1937	Headstone: _marble_ Footstone: _marble_ Artwork: _lamb lying down_ Grave Decorations: _none_
Leslie L. MITCHELL 1931-1934	Headstone: _gray granite_ Footstone: _none_ Artwork: _open gates_ Grave Decorations: _rocks placed around headstone_
Copy inscription exactly as carved on tombstone	Headstone: Footstone: Artwork: Grave Decorations:
	Headstone: Footstone: Artwork: Grave Decorations:
	Headstone: Footstone: Artwork: Grave Decorations:
	Headstone: Footstone: Artwork: Grave Decorations:
	Headstone: Footstone: Artwork: Grave Decorations:

to an issue in its file: letters requesting articles, articles, news items, correspondence, etc. Maintain a separate file drawer (which may grow into a full cabinet before you know it) or crate just for the newsletter files.

One of your first tasks as editor and, no doubt, publisher is to establish a production schedule and deadlines.

Deadline Number One

This is the writer's deadline and the one where all material for a particular issue should be on your desk. At this stage, you read all the material, edit manuscripts and enter them into your computer.

Step By Step

Deadline Number Two

If you are fortunate enough to have someone to help you copyedit (people who look over the manuscript to catch problems you may have missed when editing it), then this is the date when you need to get all the material to that person. When I edited the *Association of Professional Genealogists Quarterly*, a thirty-two-page journal, I had two copyeditors. For *Speak!* (an eight-page newsletter), I had one. Set a due date for the copyeditors to have the material back to you. Depending on the manuscript length, I try to give copyeditors ten days to two weeks.

Deadline Number Three

Once the articles have been altered (edited), they should go back to the writers by this deadline for approval. In the editing process, you or a copyeditor may have inadvertently changed the author's meaning. That's not your intention. The author is given the opportunity to correct errors created during editing. Set another deadline when changes and corrections are due back from the writers. Then make adjustments to your copy based on any changes the writer has made.

Deadline Number Four

If you are doing your own layout and design, this deadline may be when you begin formatting the issue. If someone else is doing the layout, this is when that person can expect everything on a disk.

Deadline Number Five

After the issue is formatted, it needs to go to one or more proofreaders. Even if you do not have a copyeditor on staff, **it is *essential* for you to have at least one proofreader.** By the time you get to this stage, the material in the magazine is so familiar to you—or it should be—that, not only are you sick of reading it, but it will be more difficult for you to catch errors. Don't get me wrong; you should still proofread the pages, but a fresh pair of eyes will spot mistakes that you will miss. Give your proofreaders a week or two to get the issue back to you.

Important

Deadline Number Six

After final corrections are made, it's time to print camera-ready pages to take to the printer. If you are in charge of a small newsletter, this may be simply taking the pages to a quick-copy place and photocopying them yourself. Set a deadline for the printer to have the issues ready to distribute. If you have been working with the same printer, you can give them a copy of your production schedule so they know when to expect your magazine.

Deadline Number Seven

This is the date you expect to turn over the newsletter to the post office. Though national, commercial magazines have the September issue on the newsstands in August, my feeling is that the September issue should arrive in people's mailboxes in September—even if it's the last day of September (although I must confess that on more occasions than I'd like to admit, the September issue has arrived in October). Keep in mind that the class of mail used will determine how long it could take to get the newsletter to your readers.

Deadline Number Eight

Take one day—and one day only—to relax. If you are managing and editing a quarterly issue, your deadlines may overlap. You can't be a slacker. The cycle repeats itself.

Here is a sample production schedule, based on a quarterly newsletter, with lots of time built in for all of these deadlines to occur. This newsletter is mailed first class, so there is less time built in for mailing than if it were sent second class. You can adjust your publishing schedule accordingly.

Keep in mind that the 10 January deadline for the March issue is when the articles are expected to be on the editor's desk. Soliciting people to write the articles needs to take place several months prior to that date. Once

SPEAK! PRODUCTION SCHEDULE

Issue	All material in	To copyeditors	To authors for approval	Begin formatting	To proofreaders	To printer	In mail
March	10 Jan	20 Jan	1 Feb	10 Feb	1 Mar	15 Mar	25 Mar
June	10 Apr	20 Apr	1 May	10 May	1 June	15 June	25 Jun
Sept	10 July	20 July	1 Aug	10 Aug	1 Sept	15 Sept	25 Sept
Dec	10 Oct	20 Oct	1 Nov	10 Nov	1 Dec	15 Dec	25 Dec

you have a production schedule with deadlines in place, putting together a newsletter will go much smoother.

Record Abstracting Projects

Deciding to take on a record abstracting project is another wonderful way to make a contribution to the field of genealogy. I thank every person who has undertaken this kind of project and made the results available for me to use. Naturally, you want your abstracts and publication to be as accurate as possible.

As discussed in chapter four, when you abstract a record, you copy the important aspects of the document, omitting the legal mumbo jumbo. Some genealogists choose to abstract all the wills or deeds in a particular county for a certain time period. For this project, a laptop computer is almost required. (Blessed are those who did this type of project before laptops!) Otherwise, you will be abstracting by hand, then coming home and typing the information. Every time you recopy something, you risk making more errors. After you have defined your goal and project limitations, then begin abstracting.

Documentation (citing the source of each abstract), is vital to any project, but especially an abstracting project. Researchers have to be able to find the original document from which you made the abstract. It's not that they don't trust your abstracting abilities, it's just good genealogical research practice to always look at the original.

Important

As with a cemetery project, it is better to keep the arrangement of the abstracts in the order in which the records appear in the original. Do not put them in alphabetical order thinking it will save you from making an index. You won't be doing yourself or anyone else any favors. Many a research problem has been solved by looking at the records before or after the one created by an ancestor. If you destroy that order, you may destroy someone's ability to sort through a tough research problem.

For all projects, you want to back up the project's computer files after every session when you work on the project. Though it is a time-consuming task, you should proof your copy against the originals after you abstract documents. Since you have been working with the original documents, have a friend read the abstract out loud so you can compare it to the original.

Lineage Society Applications

Lineage society applications require you to document several generations, starting with you and working on a line backward in time. You may have to deal with as many as eight or ten generations of ancestors, depending on the society to which you are applying.

Usually the society will give you a worksheet. Use it and fill in the information you know or already have. When you submit the application, lineage societies want photocopies of documents (sometimes certified copies) grouped and labeled according to each generation, so it is best to organize your working materials the way you will compile the application. Create file folders for each generation, labeling them with the generation number on the application and the names of the couples. Place in the folders proof for each couple's births, marriages and deaths, and include records to prove a connection from one generation to the next. As you acquire the proof, place a red check mark on your worksheet by each piece of information for which you have a source. When you've checked off every fact, you are ready to compile the application and send it.

Read the society's instructions carefully and completely. One organization may want all documents copied onto legal-size paper. Another may want them arranged or bound in a certain way. For all applications, keep in temporary files duplicates of everything you send until the application has been approved. Then file the documents in your permanent files according to the filing system you have chosen.

Indexing Projects

In the world of genealogy, a book without an index gets little use. Not only are we eager to look up our ancestors' names, but we need to be able to find quickly that reference to how to order vital records. Creating an index is a project in itself. Whether it's your own project or you have decided to create an index to a source that does not have one, an indexing computer program, such as Sky Index, is the way to go. It will automatically sort and alphabetize the entries. You will still need to edit the index once you transfer it into your word processor, however, because even though the indexing program is wonderful, there are usually glitches, often operator errors. For instance, if you don't enter something exactly the same way each time, you'll end up with multiple entries for the same item.

If the project you are indexing is yours, or if you are able to photocopy the material you need to index, simply go through page by page and highlight the items you want to include in the index. If you are creating two separate indexes, e.g., surname and subject, then use two different highlighter colors. Once this is finished, you will be ready to enter the data into your computer program.

Another method to create an index is to record entries on 3" × 5" cards. Make a card for each entry, then as you encounter it on a page, record the page number on the appropriate card. Enter the information into the computer and have the computer sort the entries into alphabetical order.

Documentation

All of your projects must be fully and properly documented, generally with endnotes or footnotes. If you find that you are citing from particular sources frequently, make a separate computer file of citations only. As you need the reference, copy the entry from that file, then paste the information into your project rather than typing the same data over and over again.

Elizabeth Shown Mills's *Evidence! Citation and Analysis for the Family Historian* offers guidelines for the finer points of documentation standards,

For More Info

FOR FURTHER DISCUSSION

For more on the finer points of indexing, consult Patricia Law Hatcher and John V. Wylie's *Indexing Family Histories* (see bibliography, page 130), which discusses indexing software, as well.

but basically keep in mind that you need to record all the pertinent information that will allow someone to find that source. Below are details you need to cite for books and articles. Remember, the format of the citation depends on whether it is in a note or in a bibliography. For methods of citing specific original documents, such as deeds, censuses, vital records, etc., consult *Evidence! Citation and Analysis for the Family Historian.*

For More Info

Book
- Author
- Title
- Publication place
- Publisher
- Publication date

Example used in a bibliography (no specific page numbers cited):

Hatcher, Patricia Law. *Producing a Quality Family History.* Salt Lake City: Ancestry, 1996.

Example used in a footnote or endnote (specific page numbers cited):

Patricia Law Hatcher, *Producing a Quality Family History* (Salt Lake City: Ancestry, 1996), 36-40.

Article
- Author
- Title of article
- Title of periodical
- Volume number of periodical
- Issue of periodical
- Page number(s)

Example used in a bibliography, citing inclusive pages:

Sturdevant, Katherine Scott. "Documentary Editing for Family Historians." *Association of Professional Genealogists Quarterly* 5 (Fall 1990): 51-57.

Example used in a footnote or endnote, citing a specific page reference:

Katherine Scott Sturdevant, "Documentary Editing for Family Historians," *Association of Professional Genealogists Quarterly* 5 (Fall 1990): 55.

OTHER PROJECTS

Regardless of the project you undertake, think about the project in total: your goals and how you plan to achieve them. Devise methods to keep the project organized. If a method isn't working, try something else. Ask other genealogists how they would envision organizing such a project, or ask someone who has already tackled a similar project. Researching is generally the fun part of any project, so keep your organizational method as simple as you can.

Above all, never, ever put away a work in progress. Once it gets filed, you'll never take it out again. Start a separate filing crate for each project. If you find you are overwhelmed with crates, then you know you like starting a project, you just don't like finishing it.

For all projects, keep a log of when and for how long you worked. This will be a good reference for the next time you take on a similar project. Also, as you are working on the project or soon after you complete it, make a list of things you would do differently. Keep these lists, regardless of the project, in one file folder labeled "Genealogy Projects: If I Had to Do It Over Again." On each list, put the name of the project, the starting date and ending date. A list may simply say, "Don't ever tackle this kind of project again!" Make sure you look at the file folder before you embark on any new endeavor.

SEVEN

There's More to Organize Than Your Research

T his may come as a surprise to you, but genealogists gather more than research notes and documents. Walk into any genealogist's house and you will see maps; conference lecture audiotapes; computer disks and CD-ROMs; audiotapes and videotapes of oral history interviews; notes, handouts and syllabi from conferences, seminars and classes; books and periodicals; genealogical catalogs; microforms; and tombstone rubbings. Does this give you second thoughts about this hobby? First let's look at how to organize and keep track of all this stuff. In the next chapter, we'll figure out where you're going to put everything.

COMPUTER DISKS AND CD-ROMS

There are probably very few genealogists today *not* using a computer—a desktop and/or a laptop model. Most use some kind of genealogical software program to organize data on ancestors. This information is then stored on the computer's hard drive or on disks. If you store only on your hard drive and do not back up the information on disks, you are playing with fire! My hard drive crashed two days after I finished the first draft of this book. Thankfully, I had backed up the book file to a floppy after every writing session. But I hadn't backed up my other data files in three or four months. With help from my husband, I was fortunate to be able to back up all my data files onto a Zip disk before he replaced the hard drive. A Zip disk stores 100mb; whereas a floppy stores between 1.0mb and 1.44mb. If you create a backup disk, make sure you write protect it so it can not get overwritten accidentally.

Disk storage is generally easy: You buy a disk holder. But what is on those disks? Give each document a descriptive file name; label each disk with an equally descriptive title. Make separate disks for separate activities. For example, here are labels for some of my disks:
- Articles
- Lectures

- DeBartolo Research
- Certification Renewal Items
- Organizing Book
- Stuart: Three-Generation Project
- Lesson Plans
- Reunions Columns
- Cemetery Project
- Correspondence

Tip

ORGANIZING CONFERENCE LECTURE TAPES AND SYLLABI

I undertook a project for publication of indexing the national conferences and syllabi and cataloging the lectures that were taped. This is updated each time there is a conference and will be available on the Internet via the National Genealogical Society and Federation of Genealogical Societies Web pages.

When I purchase conference lecture tapes, I enter them alphabetically by lecturer into a list I created in my word processor. This is updated each time I get a new batch of tapes, printed out, punched and placed in a three-ring binder.

—Joy Reisinger, CG

On my hard drive, I have corresponding subdirectories or folders within my word processor's directory. Most word processors today will allow you to give long descriptive file names. Take advantage of that ability. Consider including in your file name the date it was created (of course, you can look this up in the file manager, but this gives you a quick reference). This is particularly helpful for correspondence: "Ltr to Joyce Milburn 5 Feb 1996."

Just as you will purge your paper files once a year, you should also purge your computer files, either deleting old ones or moving them to floppies. But watch out! Soon you will be overrun with floppies, buying diskette caddies that hold 160 disks. Just as you can live without some of the papers in your files, you won't need to keep all of your computer files. A five-year-old letter requesting a death certificate can safely be deleted, especially if you received a response. Uncluttering your computer is as tedious and time consuming as purging your paper files. I never said it was a job you would look forward to and relish. Personally, I'd rather clean toilets.

You can also discard old, unusable floppy disks. Do you still own 5¼″ floppies, but you no longer have a computer with a 5¼″ drive? Do you see a problem here? And while we're on the subject, if you still have keys to cars or houses that you no longer own, you can toss those, too.

Eliminating Computer-Related Clutter

When organizing your computer files and disks, also look at your computer instruction manuals. Many are probably outdated, even though they were just published last month and are in mint condition. Do you really need to keep them? Even used bookstores won't take them. Couldn't you use that space to store something else?

Do you still have tractor-feed paper, but you now own a laser printer? Either separate the sheets and tear off the tractor-feed strips so you can use the sheets in your laser printer, or use it as scratch paper. If you want to use the space for other items, donate the tractor-feed paper to a school or day care.

CD-ROM Organization

As more and more databases become available on CD-ROM, you will find your collection of that medium growing. Storage is as easy as for disks: Buy a CD-ROM holder, available in a variety of styles and sizes to fit your work space. When your collection of CD-ROMs gets large, you may want to arrange them alphabetically by program title, for example:

- Ancestry Genealogy Library
- Family Tree Maker
- Family Tree Maker's Family Archives: Index to Griffith's Valuation of Ireland, 1848–1864
- Periodical Source Index

This does not work for me, though. I'm more inclined to look for "Family Tree Maker's Family Archives: Index to Griffith's Valuation of Ireland, 1848–1864" under "Griffith's Valuation," so I would place it under *G*. You may put it under *I* for Ireland. Or you may file it under *O* for O'Connor, the Irish surname you're researching. Obviously, you need to arrange your collection by whatever keywords you are likely to look for.

Remember to back up your hard drive frequently, as often as once a week if you are entering a lot of new data. Do it routinely on the same day each week—perhaps trash collection day, since that's an easy one to remember. After a day of writing or entering family history data, back up your work before you shut down the computer.

A computer saves you an incredible amount of time, but it can eat up an inordinate amount of time if it crashes and you lose everything or if it gets a virus. Computer viruses can be spread by sharing floppy disks or downloading files off the Internet, and they can virtually destroy everything you've stored on your computer. You can purchase antivirus programs from any media or computer supply store. The program monitors your computer every time you turn it on and while you're using it. If it detects a virus, the program will alert you and give suggestions on what to do. If you have not invested in a virus checker, put down this book and get one now, especially if you download information from the Internet or from E-mail attachments. Opening E-mail will not transmit a computer virus, but downloading an attachment someone sends you with an E-mail can. Nasty, inconsiderate people with nothing better to do germinate new viruses daily. No antivirus program can keep up with all viruses, but you can thwart many of them if you use one.

For disks that have irreplaceable data, make a second set of backup disks, write protect them and store them away from your home: at your (or your spouse's) office, at someone else's house or in a safe-deposit box. When I write a book for a client and send the client a disk, I always let them know I am keeping a backup.

AUDIOTAPES AND VIDEOTAPES

If you have attended any national conferences, you know you can purchase audiotapes of most of the lectures that were presented. Most genealogists have a collection of these. Again, storage is easy: Buy an audiotape holder.

When you buy the conference tapes, they come in a soft plastic case. I replace these with hard plastic cases like those for prerecorded music cas-

Sources

WHERE TO GET LECTURE RECORDINGS

A company called Repeat Performance records and sells tapes of conference lectures. See the addresses appendix on page 127 for information.

settes. You can purchase empty cases at office supply stores, discount department stores or music or media stores. It is easy to put labels on the spine of hard plastic cases.

Arrange tapes alphabetically by lecture, topic or speaker, depending on which you are more likely to look for when you want to listen to the tape again. If you find your collection of conference tapes growing, you may want to make an inventory of them using a computer database that you can sort and search by speaker's name or lecture.

Oral History Tapes

Reminder

You may also have a collection of audiotapes from oral history interviews. **Remember to label the case spine with the name of the person being interviewed**, the date and the place. If there is more than one tape from an interview session, mark and arrange them in chronological order. Keep all tapes with the same individual together, regardless of when the interviews took place.

If you have made notes or a transcript of the tape, note this somewhere on the tape case or, better yet, on the tape itself: "Notes to this interview are filed in FITZHUGH: Oral History Interview." On the notes or transcript, include in the citation that the tape is in your possession. If you have made copies of the tapes for relatives, include a list with their addresses. If anything happens to your tapes, you will know who has backups.

Do the same for videocassettes you used for oral history interviews or family events and gatherings. Use descriptive labeling, make a reference on the cassette to notes or transcriptions in your files and make a backup copy. Arrange and store them in similar fashion, buying a video storage cabinet or holder. Try to store these tapes apart from your entertainment tapes.

Always punch out the tab on audiotapes and videotapes to prevent anyone from inadvertently erasing or recording over the interviews. If you plan to add more to the tape at the next family gathering, you can cover the hole with adhesive tape to do so. This extra effort is worthwhile if it protects a one-time interview with Great-Grandma.

Important

Cassettes have a life of about ten to twenty years and will deteriorate. **Always make backup copies of irreplaceable tapes.** Store them away from your home in a climate-controlled environment.

Tape Inventories

As your tape collection grows, make an inventory of oral history tapes and videos of family events and gatherings. You can use a computer database or word processor to make an inventory or use that old standby—pen and paper. Start a separate file labeled "Tape Inventory." Once or twice a year, send a copy of the inventory to a friend or relative for safekeeping or put it in a safe-deposit box or at work. (Perhaps you are noticing a pattern here. By shipping all of your irreplaceable items to relatives, you create storage space in your own home. It's far more fun to clutter someone else's home!) Also add to your inventory of tapes your books and periodicals.

BOOKS

If you have only a small shelf of books, you must be very new to genealogy. Genealogists love books. Some have more self-control than others, but it's a rare genealogist who does not have an ever growing library. Books are my one weakness (and since I don't smoke or drink or use recreational drugs, I figure I'm allowed). I have no idea how many I actually have or how much I've spent on them, and it's probably just as well. My husband would probably divorce me if he knew. I don't have as many books as some of my friends and colleagues do, but I do have a considerable library.

When you have to hunt for a particular book or unintentionally buy books you already have, it's time to organize and inventory your books. The obsessive-compulsive genealogist will use the Dewey decimal or Library of Congress system. If you have the time, go for it! Otherwise, I just arrange them by subject and skip the neat little numbers on the spines.

Everyone's library is unique based on personal interests and areas of research, but most genealogists have certain general types of books, and you can group yours accordingly:

- how-to manuals and guidebooks
- state sources, histories and guidebooks (group county histories with the corresponding state)
- atlases and gazetteers
- ethnic sources and guidebooks (include foreign histories and guides with the corresponding American ethnic group)
- general U.S. histories
- biographies
- military histories

Tip

HOW TO MAKE SURE FRIENDS RETURN BORROWED BOOKS

Like most genealogists, I find myself lending books to friends and colleagues; and everyone knows that's a dangerous habit! It's so easy for borrowers to forget that a book has not been returned; and when the lender needs a book, it's hard to remember to whom that book was lent.

Having spent a short part of my life as a librarian, I've borrowed a practice from the library field. At my local school supply store, I buy paste-on pockets and the library cards to fit them. My friends sign the card when they "check out" one of my books. When I need a book, I don't have to trust my memory as to who borrowed it and how long ago—or wonder if I have merely mislaid it somewhere. I just look in my card file of checked out books!

—Mary McCampbell Bell, CALS, CGL

Originally published in *Association of Professional Genealogists Quarterly* 4 (summer 1989): 37.

Timesaver

Inventorying Your Books

Once your library is arranged, begin an inventory. This is where a computer database comes in handy, or you can use your word processor and enter the books as you would create a bibliography. Another method is to make a card catalog using $3'' \times 5''$ index cards stored alphabetically by author or title in a recipe file box.

In addition to the standard bibliographic information (author, title, publication place, publisher and date), also enter the cost of the book. Should you ever need this inventory for insurance purposes, you will be able to calculate the cost to replace your library.

Remember to check your inventory before you buy a book. Take the list, or a portion thereof, with you for shopping sprees to the bookstore.

Since creating this inventory will be time consuming (unless you had the foresight to start one when your library was small), you may decide it is more economical to hire your teenager or a high school student once a week for a few hours to enter the data into your computer. Once you've created the inventory, it will be easy to maintain. Anytime you buy a book, before you shelve it, enter the information in your inventory.

PERIODICALS

If you are like most genealogists, you receive a monthly or bimonthly newsletter from your local society or other societies to which you belong, along with a quarterly journal, and you subscribe to a couple of genealogical magazines or journals. Keeping them neat and tidy is usually not a problem. Cardboard or plastic magazine file boxes, like libraries use, do the trick. Keep one journal title in one box in chronological order, just like libraries do.

After a few years, you may have more magazine file boxes than you have room (see chapter eight). One solution is to purge your magazines. Sort through them and tear out the articles you want to keep, or photocopy the articles, keeping the journals intact, and donate the journals to a library or give them to a friend. File articles according to locality or topic. The problem with purging is you never know where or into what record group your research may take you. The rule in genealogy is to work from the known to the unknown, and you can't know where the unknown will lead. That article on women serving in the Civil War may not be relevant to you now, but three years from today you may discover that one of your female ancestors fought disguised as a man. If you discarded the magazine and the article, you will have to track it down at a library—not the end of the world, but frustrating.

CD Source

Another solution to genealogical magazine overload is to see if any of the journals have consolidated their issues onto CD-ROM. **Currently, back issues of the *New England Historical and Genealogical Register* (1847–1994) and the *National Genealogical Society Quarterly* (1908–1997) are available on CD-ROM.** Investing in these will free up quite a bit of shelf space if you've been subscribing for many years. You can either donate your old issues to a library, pitch them or store them elsewhere.

Introduction to PERSI

Another problem is finding a particular article you remember reading in a particular magazine. While you could certainly create your own index to articles, it's not necessary. Periodical Source Index (PERSI) was created at the Allen County Public Library in Fort Wayne, Indiana, and it is **now available on CD-ROM from Ancestry, Inc. (see addresses, on page 127). If you invest in no other CD-ROM, you will get considerable use out of PERSI.** As Patricia Law Hatcher's testimonial states on the box, "If you haven't checked PERSI, you haven't done your research—period." PERSI will tell you if someone else has already researched an ancestral line and published it in a journal or newsletter, and it will be the index to the periodicals you collect.

CD Source

PERSI indexes more than five thousand periodicals and contains more than one million citations. You can search for articles by locality, title, name, date or subject. Before the CD-ROM was released, the information on it spanned twenty-seven volumes, and you had to go to the library to use PERSI. Now you can have your own index to the magazines and periodicals that line your shelves.

The drawback to PERSI is it does not index all names or book reviews. There have been several occasions when I have wanted to read the reviews of a particular genealogy book before I bought it. To narrow my search, I find the book in a genealogical vendor's catalog and get the publishing date. Reviews tend to appear from six to eighteen months after publication, so I begin looking in journals for the review the year it was published and the next year or two after that. Most journals list the books for review in the table of contents, or they publish an annual index in the last issue of the year.

Prioritizing Your Reading

Okay. Here's the real problem: finding the time to *read* all the magazines and journals. You may have started a stack on your coffee table or by your bed of those you need to read. Ever notice that the stack gets bigger and never smaller? Here's where self-stick notes are valuable. When you receive a magazine, look through it as soon as possible. Reading small news items takes little time, and these are usually the hot items with deadlines. As you flip through, flag the longer articles you want to read when you have the time, then put the magazine in the appropriate file box.

I know what you're thinking: If the magazine is put away, you will never pull it back out and read it, right? Let me ask you this: Are you reading them now? When you buy books do you stack them by your bedside until you have the chance to read them? Of course not. You put them on your shelf until you have the time or are in the mood to read them. Why not do the same with magazines?

Because the article titles are not visible like the spine of a book to jar your memory, **start an article reading list (see the Article Reading List form on page 143).** As you flag the article, jot down on your list the title or subject of the article, the abbreviated journal name and date of the issue. You don't need the page number, since the page is flagged. Post the list on

A Useful Form You Can Reproduce
For a full-sized blank copy of the Article Reading List form, see page 143. You are free to photocopy this form for personal use.

your refrigerator, your bulletin board or the bathroom mirror—someplace where you will see it and use it. When you travel or have a doctor's appointment (where you *know* you will have to wait), check your list for articles you feel like reading, and take one or two magazines with you. For information and encouragement, cross off the articles as you read them.

Keep one or two journals in your car to make good use of your time when you unexpectedly have to wait. Instead of thumbing through an ancient copy of *Reader's Digest*, you can read your magazine. Do not, however, let all of your magazines pile up in your car! This merely transfers "the stack." Only put one or two in the car and replace them only when you have finished reading the articles you have flagged.

Fortunately, it doesn't matter whether you read genealogical articles today, tomorrow or two years from now. They generally aren't time sensitive.

GENEALOGICAL AND BOOK CATALOGS

If you're not on all the major genealogical vendor mailing lists, now's the time to sign up. Send a postcard, fax or E-mail to the addresses in the back of this book (see page 127). Not that you need more things to organize and file, but once you start receiving the catalogs you will see what books there are to research and, perhaps, buy. The catalogs are easily stored like magazines. You will need one or two magazine file boxes, depending on the number of catalogs you receive and want to keep. I have one magazine box for genealogical vendor catalogs and another for nongenealogical vendor book catalogs, such as university press catalogs. To keep catalogs under control, throw away an old one when the new issue arrives. You can arrange them alphabetically within the boxes.

From the catalogs, make two lists: books you want to buy for your collection and books you want to check the next time you're at a research library (see the Book Wish List and Research Checklist of Books forms on pages 144 and 145).

CONFERENCE AND SEMINAR MATERIALS

When you attend a genealogical conference or seminar, you will usually get syllabi or handout materials to accompany the speakers' lectures. Take notes right on the handouts or in the syllabi. Taking notes on separate sheets leaves you with some problems: You have to decide what to do with the notes (keep them folded in the syllabus or file them), and you run a greater risk of the notes getting lost or mislaid.

If you receive a bound syllabus, treat it as a book, include it on your inventory and shelve it. If you receive loose handouts, make a file with the name and date of the seminar and file them. You may want to combine your seminar notes and handouts into files or binders and arrange by topic, e.g., "Irish research" or "census research."

Every conference you attend will likely give you a "goodie bag." About

90 percent of the goodies you can pitch; do this as soon as possible. Do not bring all this stuff home with you to sort.

Usually, you can pick up many flyers or brochures from vendors or tables. Be selective and take only flyers you need. If a vendor insists you take a flyer that you don't want, be polite and do so, then discreetly pitch it. Any literature you take home you should promptly organize and file.

GENEALOGICAL CLASS AND WORKSHOP MATERIALS

Genealogical instructors expect that you will take notes, and they will give you handouts. Unless the instructor gives you another idea for storing all this paper and bringing it to class, buy a three-ring binder and subject dividers. Genealogical courses generally last from four to fifteen weeks; use one subject divider for each class session. Keep your notes and handouts for that session behind a divider labeled either by date or topic.

Genealogical workshops are usually held for one day. Depending on the number of handouts you receive and notes you take, either use a ½″ binder or a file folder for them, and label it with the workshop name and date.

TOMBSTONE RUBBINGS

Aside from displaying tombstone rubbings on the walls of your living room, family room, bathroom, bedroom and laundry room, you will want to keep a record of them and store them properly. If you have not done so already, make a note on your family group sheet or in your SURNAME: Cemetery Records file that you have a rubbing of a particular tombstone. You can also have poster-size photocopies of the rubbing made at a quick-print shop for family Christmas gifts or to keep as backups.

Somewhere on the rubbing (usually the back), record all the pertinent information: a transcription of the information from the stone, the name and location of the cemetery, the location of the grave marker and the date the rubbing was made. This data should also be recorded in your files.

Now decide where to put them. Remember, tombstone rubbings are family artifacts and should be treated as such. One hundred years from now, the stone may no longer be legible, but your rubbing will be. If the rubbing is on paper, consider redoing it on fabric the next time you visit that cemetery. Nonfusible interfacing fabric is inexpensive and will last far longer than paper, especially newsprint. Butcher paper is sturdier, but it, too, is prone to tear. Interfacing fabric is used to make collars and cuffs stiff. It can be purchased in quantity at any fabric store. I use medium to heavy weight interfacing. It won't tear, it can be folded and refolded, ironed and easily stored in a box, hope chest or wherever you keep your fine linens.

Store paper rubbings in a corresponding file or a box. Keep in mind that every time you unfold and refold, you weaken the paper at the crease. Instead of folding, roll them and put them into cardboard mailing tubes or old wrapping paper tubes. Place sheets of butcher or tissue paper in between

Tip

FREEBIES ARE YOUR FRIENDS!

I pick up almost anything and everything from a freebie table at a conference or library or any other facility that has handouts, especially ones that have maps on them. Usually these items have some useful content. Sometimes they are advertisements for some printed source that is relative to my work and areas of specialization. Sometimes it is something that gives me a new idea. All of these freebies go into a three-ring binder based on content. If they can't help me, they might help a student, client, friend or colleague.

—Jonathan D. Galli, CGRS

each rubbing to prevent them from smearing on one another. You can probably fit two or three in one tube. Like folding, however, unrolling paper that has become brittle over time will eventually ruin a rubbing.

MAPS

I love being a member of AAA (American Automobile Association). I get all the free maps I want. These are already folded, so they store nicely. Arrange them in alphabetical order. Cardboard file boxes for business-size checks are a convenient place to file folded maps. You can also use small magazine file boxes or recycle boxes that business-size envelopes come in. To store unfolded maps, roll them and put them in mailing tubes or old wrapping paper tubes.

Some maps you will want to store flat. Use wall space or the backs of doors to keep them within sight. Or place the maps between two pieces of poster board or cardboard and store them under a bed or between a piece of furniture and a wall.

Tip

TIPS FOR FILING MAPS

No map cabinet and no place to put one even if you had it? How can you store—flat—your large collection of maps of all sizes? How can you maintain a filing order so that they can be found and won't be needlessly worn by searching through a big pile every time one map is needed?

I use large sheets of poster board to create giant file folders, taping two sheets together to make a front, a back and a hinge. Each folder can then be labeled and stacked in whatever order I choose. When a map from a certain area or time frame is needed, I have only a few folders to go through instead of a lot of loose sheets. I can easily retrieve the appropriate folder without damaging my entire collection by unnecessarily handling and shuffling the fragile paper that maps are printed on. When I'm through, the slick poster board folder will then easily slide back into the stack between the folders.

—Ge Lee Hendrix, CG, FASG

Originally published in *Association of Professional Genealogists Quarterly* 4 (Summer 1989): 37.

CD Source

MICROFILM AND MICROFICHE

Some genealogists own a microfilm or microfiche reader and purchase frequently used films, or they rent them from a genealogical lending library **(see addresses, page 127).** If you purchase a significant number of films,

Tip

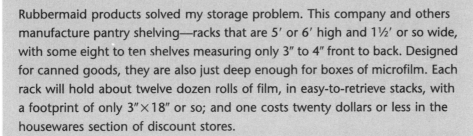

TIPS FOR MICROFILM STORAGE

My home office is typical of those of many genealogists: It was once an extra bedroom that I have converted to office use. It contains a microfilm reader and seemingly zillions of rolls of film. The room is not large enough to accommodate the film, much less a microfilm cabinet.

Rubbermaid products solved my storage problem. This company and others manufacture pantry shelving—racks that are 5' or 6' high and 1½' or so wide, with some eight to ten shelves measuring only 3" to 4" front to back. Designed for canned goods, they are also just deep enough for boxes of microfilm. Each rack will hold about twelve dozen rolls of film, in easy-to-retrieve stacks, with a footprint of only 3"×18" or so; and one costs twenty dollars or less in the housewares section of discount stores.

So where do you put these inelegant tiers of film? In the closet of the converted bedroom, of course. My three racks fit perfectly, flat against the center of the back wall, behind the old clothes pole and between the built-in shelves that are fitted into each side wall of the closet for supply storage. (Sears also has shelving units that exactly fit the depth of most closets.) A microfilm cabinet to hold five hundred reels can easily cost five hundred dollars. Mine costs less than fifty dollars and eats up none of the floor space that we genealogists never have enough of!

—Elizabeth Shown Mills, CG, FASG

Originally published in *Association of Professional Genealogists Quarterly* 4 (summer 1989): 37.

you will need to find a storage place for them. After you have labeled microfilm boxes with descriptive titles, you can arrange them by record type or locality. There are several ways to store boxes of microfilm:

- Use a 4"×6" card file cabinet
- Use a video cabinet to store microfilm and videos together
- Use a canceled check file box (these are 9" wide, so you can store two rows side by side)
- Use a computer media drawer (if it holds Zip disk cases, it will be the right dimensions for a microfilm box)

Microfiche fits perfectly in a 4"×6" card file box or cabinet. Each microfiche sheet usually comes in its own paper jacket. Arrange these by subject.

After you find a convenient storage container, the next challenge is finding a place for it. What a great subject for the next chapter!

EIGHT

Finding Room in Your House for Your Genealogy Stuff

I t all boils down to space. There's never enough of it. Even if you moved into a bigger house or added on to your present home, I can almost guarantee that you will still run out of space. After all, when you have more room, you can get more stuff.

The best solution is to create more space by decluttering. Reevaluate everything you own regarding your genealogy. Are there things you could really live without? Are there dried up pens and highlighters in your desk? Toss them. Are there books you have read or no longer use? Donate them to a local library or trade them at a used-book store. Are there old journals and magazines you could pack up and store somewhere?

Think about the personal items that decorate your office or work area. Sure, you want to give the room your own identity, and I'm not suggesting you depersonalize your office, but there are little things you can do to create space. Do you really need potted plants that sit on a desk, shelf, or the top of a filing cabinet? Decorate with hanging plants instead. Keep only books and journals relevant to genealogy on your work area's bookshelves; move the novels and other reading materials to another room. Keep knickknacks to a minimum; they are just more things to dust anyway. Pictures of the family on your desk? Hang the pictures on a wall, or move them to another room. Take a critical look at every item in your office, and ask yourself whether it has to be right there in your office.

YOUR WORK AREA

Most of us begin doing genealogy on the kitchen or dining room table. We like to spread out our charts and have room to work. The dining room table seemed like the perfect place until it was time for dinner. Then everything you were working on had to be packed up and put away.

With the popularity of desktop computers, many people have already converted a spare room or part of the dining or living room into a work area. This is good, but you still need room to spread things out. You also need a space that is totally yours, where you don't have to hunt for scissors, pens, paper or any other office supplies. Once family members see all the neat stuff you have, the kids will want some colored paper and folders, too, your spouse will need to use your copy machine just this once, and you'll find your pens and notepads in other rooms of the house. If you must, buy duplicates of the less-expensive sought-after items so family members can have their own. Buy exact duplicates—a substitute item will never do. The child in everyone simply won't accept substitutes—or the problem will continue.

If you don't have a spare room to claim for your genealogy, the next choice is to kick one of the kids out of a bedroom. He or she will be leaving soon for college anyway. (Just because the child is only six and still has twelve years to live at home, you should not let this influence you. It's time to bunk with a sibling and learn what dorm life is all about.) Perhaps a friend or neighbor will take in your child as an apprentice, providing room and board. It worked in colonial times. Frankly, confining your genealogy to just one room will be a challenge in itself. The overflow will eventually creep into other rooms without you even realizing it.

IF YOU DON'T HAVE AN OFFICE

If there is simply no room in the house for you to have a separate genealogy room, you will have to keep your stuff to a minimum. Try to create an area that is your territory, though. One way to do this is to purchase a folding screen to establish an area of the living room or a bedroom that will be all yours. If space is really limited, consider purchasing a cabinet-style computer desk. This is similar to an old secretary where the piece folds up and looks like a cabinet when not in use. When opened, you have your work area.

Another possibility is to take over the largest closet in the house and make it into a work area. You can build shelves and have a stationary or fold-up table attached to one wall (like a fold-up ironing board or a Murphy bed) on which to work. If all else fails and there just isn't any room, you can always put your bed on pulleys and raise it to the ceiling when you want to work on your genealogy.

If you don't have a computer or if you have a family computer, consider purchasing a laptop just for your genealogical pursuits. With a laptop you can create a genealogist's nook just about anywhere—even in the bathroom, if you're so inclined—and a laptop will be a great advantage to you when you are out and about doing research.

Avoid buying books if space is limited. Buy only those you absolutely need, like guidebooks. For all others, use the library's copies or join a society, like the National Genealogical Society or the New England Historic Genealogical Society, which have lending libraries **(see addresses, page 127).**

Keep your files in portable file boxes or crates that you can stack in a

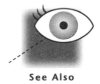

See Also

corner or in a closet. Purge your files regularly to keep your files down to one or two crates. A filing crate on wheels will increase your choices of where to keep it, since you can easily move it to where you want to work.

Limit the number of journals and magazines to which you subscribe. You can read these at the genealogical library, too, even though it is not as relaxing as curling up in your favorite chair.

Use the kitchen or dining room table; purchase TV trays for eating. Be sure to get enough trays to seat everyone in the family and for those times you want to entertain (dinner parties and holidays). Perhaps you should move to a climate where you can eat outside year-round on a patio or picnic table.

In essence, utilize and occupy every space in every room of the house for your genealogy. Say good-bye to any fancy decorating scheme (American Southwest, French Provincial, Early Americana); you and your family may as well get used to the I'm-Hopelessly-Hooked-on-Genealogy decor.

IF YOU DO HAVE AN OFFICE

As mentioned, the size of the spare room you're occupying doesn't matter. You will fill it regardless. Setting up a work space is a personal matter; what works for you may not work for another. The U-shaped setup is the most popular. That's how my office is arranged (see the diagram on page 95). Along one wall is a 6' folding table. Next to it is my computer desk. On the perpendicular wall is a secretarial desk I picked up at a used office furniture store. The other leg of the U is where the secretarial desk extends and my typewriter sits. My office chair is on wheels, so I can easily move from the computer desk to the secretarial desk. Purchase plastic office mats to place on the carpet so your chair glides easily.

While everyone wants to have everything right at their fingertips, this is nearly impossible. Consider what reference sources you use most frequently (dictionary, citation manual, etc.) and keep those items within reach. Genealogists tend to sit too much anyway (at a desk, behind the computer, in front of a microfilm reader), so getting up to retrieve something helps the circulation.

THE MESSY DESK SYNDROME

It's your desk. You can keep it as neat or as messy as you like. But if you lose things and can't find things on your desk, you may want to consider straightening it up just a bit.

Hugh Kenner, author of the essay "The Untidy Desk and the Larger Order of Things," believes in the "80-20 rule": you use 20 percent of the items in your office 80 percent of the time. "So," he writes, "if 20 percent of the contents of the room is piled on your desk instead of being stowed in the out-of-sight places where clean-deskers try to tell you it 'belongs,'

Notes

USING EVERY SPACE

I have grown out of my office at home and hate to think about the day I will have to take my files and books from my newspaper office to the house. The cat may not like it, but we are planning to take over her room, which is a tiny room off my home office. In it we will build wall-to-wall bookshelves. I'll move the file cabinets and a small study table there. This will allow me to spread out in my actual office area without adding on to the house or disrupting another room.
—Regina Hines Ellison, CGRS

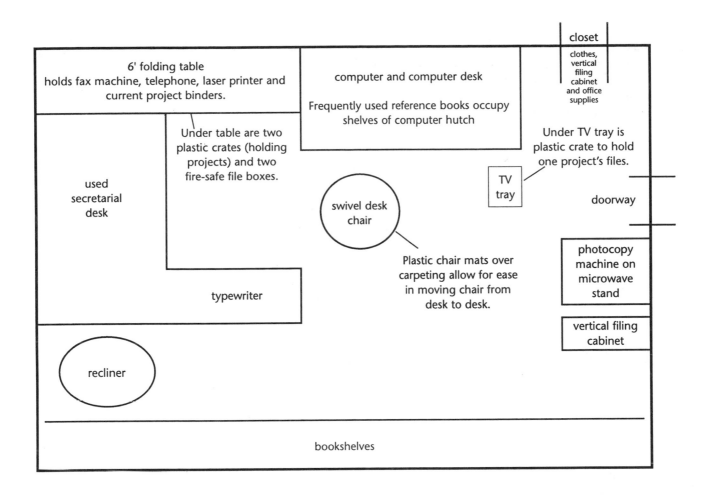

then 80 percent of your needs can be satisfied by what's instantly within reach from where you sit."

Think in terms of kitchen spices. You may have a whole cabinet full of spices, but you probably only use 20 percent of them: salt, pepper, garlic powder, cinnamon. No doubt these are kept toward the front of the cabinet because you use them frequently. But how often do you use saffron or marjoram leaves? These get tucked way in the back, and you have to fumble for them on the few occasions when you have a recipe that calls for them.

This 80-20 rule can apply to practically anything. Think about tools. The basic tools—a straight screwdriver, a Phillips screwdriver, pliers and a hammer—are the 20 percent you use for 80 percent of the jobs. Allen wrenches and vice grips are handy to have, but you probably have more need for a screwdriver. Thus, you may have to hunt for the vice grips in your tool chest, but the screwdriver is right there on top. As Kenner says, "Use always tends to draw what is used in close."

So keeping your desk cluttered with 20 percent of the things you use the most is more productive than keeping it clutter free. The items you need today are probably the same items you will need to use tomorrow, next week or next month. It makes sense to keep them handy. This really is a more efficient way to work than putting things away all of the time and

Notes

IN DEFENSE OF MESSY DESKS

From four supervisors in a row, I have observed characteristics of messy-desk bosses as opposed to clean-desk bosses. My two messy-desk bosses incrementally stacked papers, books, files, reports and anything else handed to them in teetering piles that extended across, forward and back and vertically from their desks. These piles only grew, unless or until a secretary could stand them no more. They appeared to be as stable and well organized as an avalanche waiting to happen.

My two clean-desk bosses would spread only those papers they were using each day, cautiously, within a central section of their desks. At the end of each day, they would clear their desks completely. One of these two learned this as a habit from years in military intelligence, where security required him to leave his desk empty. The other clean-desk boss formed the habit by choice, boasted of it, and belittled messy-desk people.

Both messy-desk bosses could lay their hands on anything promptly, even if they pulled it from the middle of precarious piles. When other people could not find something because they had discarded their copies, the messy-desk bosses were often the only ones who still had accessible copies. After all, they kept everything, as they received it, in a sort of chronological order of sedimentary layers. The messy-desk bosses, because they would not worry about petty bureaucratic matters, tended to be fascinating people with sharp minds, eclectic interests and humane spirits. They rebelled against stupidity and authoritarianism.

The two clean-desk bosses usually found missing documents by asking their secretary. While these bosses had been discarding papers in order to clean house every day, the secretary had been maintaining two archives—theirs and her own. Of course—you guessed it—the secretary was a messy-desk person, making her indispensable. The military man was well intentioned but a company man, right or wrong. The clean-desk boss who was that way by choice lost the most documents and had difficulty keeping track of many important matters. She was submissive to authority, even during its moments of stupidity, and careless of others, often in very detrimental ways. But her desk was always clean.

Four people do not a scientific sample make, of course. If, however, like me, you are something of a messy-desk person, take heart! It may mean that you are better organized than many clean-desk people are. After all, you are well organized enough to prioritize superficial desk cleaning *lower* on your list than matters of more serious import to humanity!

—Katherine Scott Sturdevant, historian

pulling them out every time you need them. "Remember," Kenner says, "it is *total* effort that we're trying to minimize." I don't care what the authors of other books on organizing tell you about striving for a clutter-free environment. I agree with Kenner and the 80-20 rule. Twenty percent clutter is more efficient and productive than no clutter.

ROLODEX OR ADDRESS BOOK?

I use a Rolodex card file and an address book. The Rolodex stays on my desk, and the address book travels with me. Yes, it's duplication, but if I lose the address book, I can reconstruct it with the information on the Rolodex.

Nowadays, if you are using or planning to buy an address book, make sure it has enough fields for all the various information people have:

- name
- street address
- mailing address
- phone number
- fax number
- pager number (digital and/or voice message)
- Mobile phone number
- E-mail address
- Web address

Incredible isn't it—all the ways to contact someone? Makes it hard to really get away from it all, too.

Besides simply organizing your Rolodex alphabetically by names, you can organize by topics, then alphabetically by names:

- libraries and research repositories
- genealogical and historical societies
- professional genealogists
- books on loan
- clients
- local bookstores
- office supply stores
- genealogical vendors

Another method of keeping track of all your contacts is to utilize the address book function that's a feature of many word processors. This is particularly handy when you need to do mass mailings or make labels. Keep a backup copy in case your computer crashes. Some electronic organizers (PalmPilot by 3Com is one) allow you to link with your desktop or laptop computer to continually update these lists and allow you to take the information with you when you travel.

Tip

USING AN ADDRESS BOOK INSTEAD OF A ROLODEX

I hate Rolodexes. They take up precious desk space. I prefer an address book that I can put in a drawer or on a bookshelf. Plus, the address book I can take with me when I travel.

I purchased a loose-leaf address book with plastic, pocketed pages just the right size for business cards. I used to enter the information from the card into a former address book then throw away the cards. But now all I have to do is slip the card into one of the pockets. Each plastic page holds six cards. It is easy to move the cards around in the pockets, so I can organize them in any order.
—Roger D. Joslyn, CG, FASG

WHERE SHALL I PUT ALL THIS EQUIPMENT?

The bare necessities for most genealogists are a desktop computer and a printer. You may also have a scanner and Zip drive. As you get more addicted to genealogy, you may decide you cannot live without a desktop photocopy machine or a fax or a microfilm reader or a microfiche reader. These are not small items; they take up lots of room. While it is nice to have them all in the same room, is it really necessary? My photocopy machine I use frequently, so it is in my office on a microwave stand. The shelf and cabinet below are perfect for holding reams of paper and blank overhead transparencies. If I didn't have room in my office for it, I could easily put it in another room. On the other hand, I don't use my microfilm and fiche readers often, so they sit on an old kitchen table in the basement.

A PLACE FOR EVERYTHING AND EVERYTHING IN ITS PLACE

In chapter seven, I gave you ideas on how to store things such as microforms, audiotapes, videotapes and computer disks. The real challenge is finding a place to put all those nifty storage boxes and holders. Since I cannot see your house, the best I can do is speak in general terms and make suggestions.

Shelves are always a good idea. If the spare room has a closet that you can use, put shelves in it. This is also a good place to store office supplies.

Another spot is under desks. Of course, you need to have room for your legs and feet, but there is usually some dead space where you can store a box of file folders or envelopes. Under my 6' table, I have two file crates and two fire-safe file boxes. Anything I don't get into that often can go way in the back.

Remember, everything does *not* have to be right at your fingertips. Put some items in another room, under the bed, in a closet, in the basement or in the attic.

Think of your office as different areas. In the area where your copy machine stands, store supplies for that function: copier paper, toner cartridges, user's manual. In your computer area, keep items such as disks, CD-ROMs and manuals. In the area where you make and receive phone calls, keep phone books, pens, message pads and an address book or Rolodex.

Thumb through office supply catalogs. These will give you ideas on ways to store things. Look at how other genealogists arrange their work space. Look in the yellow pages for a professional organizer and ask them what the cost would be to have someone come to your home for a consultation. There may also be classes on organizing offered at a community college or a community center.

MOVING YOUR GENEALOGY AND OFFICE

You just got your office set up the way you like it and found the perfect place for everything. Now it's time to move to a new home.

MORE MOVING TIPS

We learned several things from our move. Every piece of delicate equipment should have been moved by us. The glass screen on our overhead projector was demolished, and the movers somehow bent the frame that holds the glass pieces on a microfilm reader. The lenses on the reader were scratched and chipped, but are still usable; however, the film won't slide between the glass.

If I could give anyone advice, it would be to plan in advance for furniture placement within your office. Have the floor cleaned and be ready to tell the movers exactly where to set the desks, files cabinets and bookcases.

We used to have our desks in front of the bookcases so we could turn around and reach the most often used sources. Now we put the file cabinets within arm's reach because we found that we went to the files more often than the books.

I would also advise genealogists to pack and label the contents of their file cabinets. The movers can tilt the cabinets, with contents, onto a dolly and move them, but this is treacherous when stairs are involved, and cabinets are heavy at any location.

—Marty Hiatt, CGRS

Adapted from *Association of Professional Genealogists Quarterly* 9 (June 1994): 36-37.

I had the "joy" of moving twice within a four-month period; both times were right before I spoke at national conferences. (My therapist says the results of the combined stresses of these events should have no real lasting effects, and I am getting better; I only have to wear the straitjacket at night now!) The first move (packed and transported by us) was across town; the second move (packed and transported by the company) was to another town, forty-five miles away. Surprisingly, the post office kept up well with my changes of address.

For the first move, packing my office myself was time consuming, but worth the effort. I was able to label boxes precisely as to the contents, so unpacking was relatively painless. For the second move, the moving company packed, and I thoroughly enjoyed sitting on the couch, watching TV and eating Oreos (until they packed the TV and I ran out of cookies). Then came time to *un*pack. The movers had only two categories for my office item boxes: books or files. I felt terribly disorganized when I was sorting and unpacking these boxes; the setup of my office, therefore, took twice as long as when I had packed it myself. Fortunately, we had saved the original boxes and packing material for all of my office equipment (computer, printer, copy machine) and packed these items ourselves for both moves;

the moving company only transported them. (It's also important to save these original boxes in case you need to return an item still under warranty.)

The self-packed move resulted in almost no damage; the mover-packed one was much different. There was no major damage, just little things—like files being packed upside down or other items stacked on top of them, crushing the tabs. This was annoying, to say the least. I was able to claim several boxes worth of file folders on the damage report, but money to replace the folders does not compensate for the time to redo the files. Some of my paperback books had bent covers when I unpacked them. Obviously, someone else is not going to be as careful with your things as you would be.

My genealogy downtime was about four to six weeks per move. For the self-packed move, the bulk of the downtime was spent packing; for the professional move, the bulk of the downtime was spent unpacking.

Change of Address

It helped immensely to have a list of all the names and addresses of societies, subscriptions and other mailings when I moved and had to send change-of-address cards. Start a computer address book in your word processor (mail merge), so you can easily make labels on your computer and affix them to change-of-address cards. This list will also be valuable should you need to do other mass mailings, for example, a letter announcing that you are seeking information for a book you are compiling or a prepublication announcement for a book on your family history.

Tip

PACKING BOOKS AND OFFICE EQUIPMENT

For a long-distance move, books should be sorted by size and should be packed tightly in one-and-a-half-cubic foot boxes (a standard size sold by the movers), with as many of the books as possible stacked flat. Packing the books vertically, especially with spines up, can lead to broken spines and warped books. Sorting by size adds some time at both ends of the move but helps protect the books.

Although I did not make a careful inventory of the contents of each box, I did label them roughly (e.g., "Genealogies," "New England History"), so that as the movers unloaded them in New Hampshire, I could direct them to the correct room.

I have one special rule that looks ahead to future moves: Never throw away the box that something comes in. Whether it is your laser printer or your desktop postal scales or your bedside clock radio, preserving the original packing will save time and nuisance when it comes to moving.

—Robert Charles Anderson, CG, FASG

Adapted from *Association of Professional Genealogists Quarterly* 9 (June 1994): 36-37.

STORAGE

As you purge your files, think about storing back issues of magazines and newsletters and other items you use infrequently. Keep the past two or three years of periodicals within easy access, but store older ones in a basement, attic or garage. Old or infrequently used files can be stored in Bankers Boxes you purchase at discount department stores or office supply stores.

If you're storing in an attic, make sure nothing can be damaged by heat. We used to store our Christmas decorations in the attic; you should see the lovely shape that Santa candle melted into. There are equal concerns if you store in a basement. If there is even the remotest possibility of flooding, put boxes on shelves or pallets. If you live in a humid climate, be careful of mildew. When we lived in Florida, I had my high school yearbook in a box in a spare bedroom. When I opened the box after our move to Colorado, mildew had eaten away many of the pages. Keep in mind that prolonged exposure to heat and humidity can damage media such as computer disks, audiotapes, videotapes, photographs and negatives.

Warning

Critters are another enemy to your genealogy items kept in storage. Creepy, crawly things that I don't even like to think about enjoy feasting on your papers and leaving ghastly droppings on them. I don't know what kind of worms they have in Italy, but every time I look at the vital records on microfilm, I can make out their little carcasses stuck to the pages—not a pleasant sight.

As you move items to storage, keep an inventory of everything in each box. My husband devised a system of numbering our boxes, using a big, black marker, on all sides and the top. He tries to keep the boxes in numerical order in the basement. The box inventory, maintained on the computer, is printed out and hung on a wall in the basement. We can either search for an item on the database or by scanning the printout.

If you decide to store valuable historical items and backup disks in a bank safe-deposit box, make sure you keep a list somewhere of what's in the box. A good place to keep the list is with your important papers, such as a will or the deed to your house, where someone can learn that the box exists and what's in it. The list also serves as a reminder for you in case you go hunting for an item you've forgotten you put in the safe-deposit box.

If you think you might want to store data on a CD-ROM so you can get rid of some of your clutter, you may want to think again. I'll tell you why in chapter ten.

NINE

Organization for Professional Genealogists

T he day you declare yourself a professional genealogist is the day you have even more paper to deal with. Congratulations. Now you have not only your own genealogy—which will take a backseat to paying clients from now on—but you also have your clients' genealogy to make room for and file. Many professional genealogists maintain two file cabinets: one for their own family history research, the other for their clients' materials.

CLIENT FILES

You must decide which you are more likely to remember when you label your client files: the name of the client or the name(s) of the client's ancestors. Some professionals put the client's name on the file tab, then list the names of the ancestors on the outside of the file folder. The extent of research you are doing for a client will determine how involved a filing system you will need. If you have been commissioned to research just one individual or family, a single file folder may suffice. If you are tracing all the client's ancestors, one file folder would not work. In this case, you may want to set up a system similar to the one you use for your own ancestry, filing by surname and type of record or by couple/family group.

For most client projects, you will need at least three files:
- a business folder to keep past billing statements and a copy of your contract with the client
- a folder of information the client initially sends you to start the project, e.g., previous reports from other researchers, photocopies of documents the client has gathered, notes on the family, etc.
- a folder of research and materials that you will generate and gather based on your research and what the client has sent you, e.g., pedigree

Tip

A CLIENT FILES TIP

On my client file folders, I write the main family names I am researching for that client on the outside of the folder. Then when someone else asks about a family, and I don't remember exactly which client I did work on that family for, I can just glance at the outside of the folders to find the one I want.

—Marie Martin Murphy, CGRS

chart, family group sheets, research plan, photocopies of documents, research reports, etc.

When I was taking research clients, most of my commissions were for short-term projects, such as tracking down everything on a particular family during their lives in Colorado. One research file folder was generally sufficient, and I took the folder with me when I went to a research facility. For long-term projects involving several generations, the files stayed at home, but I took with me a folder or binder of the bare essentials: family group sheet(s), pedigree charts, research plan, my last report to the client and abstracts of previously acquired documents.

The longer you are in business, the more clients and folders you will generate. Most professional genealogists keep a copy of *everything* they acquire and send to the client. They also keep their notes from which the research report is written.

As you close out a research project for a client or when the client calls a halt to your services, you need to decide what to do with inactive files. Few genealogists throw the contents away, but some do. They figure that if a former client rehires them, they will simply ask the client to photocopy everything and send it to them. Personally, I think this is dangerous. If the former client writes you for a copy because the house burned down or the client loaned the material to a relative who lost it, you can only help if you kept copies.

Former clients do resurface, or sometimes you will be commissioned by someone who has ancestry in common with a former client. You may also decide that the research you did for a client five years ago would be a good example to use in a class or lecture or as a sample of your work for certification or recertification (with the client's permission or removing identifying information about the client). Most professional genealogists keep all of their client files and contents, storing the inactive ones in a basement, attic, garage or off-site storage facility.

CLIENT CONTRACTS/INFORMATION SHEETS

Many genealogists have learned that it is a great time-saver and headache preventer in the long run to have all your terms written out, up front, when a client first engages your services. This can be a formal contract or simply an information sheet you have the client sign, acknowledging that they read and understood the information. Basics to include are

- your hourly fee and what it covers (analysis, research, report writing, data entry)
- how often the client can expect a report
- expenses the client is responsible for (travel, parking, photocopies, phone and fax charges, etc.)
- other client responsibilities (supplying you with previous research to avoid duplication)

For More Info

FOR FURTHER DISCUSSION

For more on this topic, see Paula Stuart Warren and James W. Warren's "Communicating With Clients Part One: The Information and Rate Sheet" in the *Association of Professional Genealogists Quarterly 7* (June 1992): 42-44.

- anticipated use of the research (for publication, to share with relatives, for personal knowledge)

For More Info

FOR FURTHER DISCUSSION

For more on this topic, see Suzanne McVetty and Roger D. Joslyn's "Tactics for Metropolitan Areas" in *Association of Professional Genealogists Quarterly* 13 (December 1998): 120-127.

CLIENT RESEARCH MANAGEMENT

As a new professional genealogist, you may have only one or two clients, so managing your research and reporting time is not complicated. When you start getting a half dozen or more clients, however, time management becomes more complex. Many professionals keep a to-do list, either by client with the names of the repositories where research needs to be done or by research repositories with the names of clients that require research in that facility. Professional genealogists Roger D. Joslyn and Suzanne McVetty make to-do lists according to the research facility they need to visit. Below the name of each research repository, they list the names of clients who need research in those facilities, followed by what they need to look for:

NYC Archives

JONES

Follow up on Isabelle Prentise in almshouse

Anything more on Toolans in VRs [vital records], etc.?

BUCHANAN

Brooklyn marriage of Edward L. O'Connor and Corinda Norris, 24 May 1920

HARRIS

brides' index for Gertrude Bryam 1900–1920; not in Brooklyn 1901–10, try Manhattan

Prioritizing client work is sometimes a challenge. As they say, "The squeaky wheel gets the grease." Squeaky clients who call frequently to check on the status of the research often get put at the top of the list—unless you have passive/aggressive tendencies, then they get put on the bottom. When I was taking clients, I placed new clients at the top of the list to get their project started. After the first report they were put at an equal level with everyone else. Other professionals I've spoken with inform new clients that their research will go on a waiting list until prior clients get their current report.

One way to prioritize clients is to have as your goal a report to each client every thirty days. Depending on the number of clients you have, this may or may not be feasible, so perhaps you will need to extend the time frame to every six weeks or every other month. Once one client is sent a report, work for that client goes to the bottom of the list. This may work better in theory than practice. There will always be clients whose research you just can't get excited about, so work for them tends to be a low priority. Usually, the client who has been waiting patiently, the one you haven't had contact with in months, starts to nag at your conscience, making you feel guilty, and then becomes your priority.

Setting Professional Priorities

Here are some things to think about when you are trying to prioritize client work:

- What kind of work are you doing for this client? Is it research you enjoy or something you are putting off? Is it a long-term or short-term project?
- Where do you need to conduct this client's research? If it's a repository you visit infrequently, then the client will probably be a low priority.
- What are the client's goals? If the client is planning to publish a book, attend a family reunion or make a trip to the ancestral site, you need to take this into consideration.
- What is the health of the client? Someone with a terminal illness should get prompt research reports.
- What is the interest and enthusiasm of the client? It's hard to get excited about research if the client has a blasé attitude.
- What other attitudes does the client project? Some clients are wonderful to work for; others are a pain. That can have a big impact on where you put that client on your to-do list.
- Does the client pay on time? You want to keep this kind of client happy at all costs.
- Does the client give you occasional bonuses? Keep this client happy, too.

New professionals often don't realize that report writing can take as much time as research, sometimes longer. If a new client has authorized five hours, for example, one hour might be taken up with initially analyzing the problem and creating a research plan, and at least one to two hours should be reserved for writing the report, leaving only two to three hours maximum for actual research time. By using a written agreement as discussed earlier, you alert the client of this aspect. If you are entering the client's data into a genealogical software program, you must also allow time for this activity.

On all notes you take for a client, make sure you record all the same information you would for your own family, including the name of the client and complete source citations. In fact, you can easily use and adapt all the same forms that you use in your personal research for client research.

REPORT WRITING

Create a separate computer file of source citations you frequently consult for your clients. You can use this bibliography of sorts not only as a checklist, but when you write reports, you can copy from the list particular citations,

Tip

KEEPING AN INDEX CARD FILE OF SOURCE CITATIONS

Once I find a new source at a local repository, I write down the title and call number on an index card. I punch a hole in the bottom corner of the index card and keep all of the cards together with a loose-leaf ring. I keep these cards in my briefcase so I have an easy reference when researching.

It may not seem necessary to write down the titles and call numbers, but I don't always use the same sources for all clients. It may be several weeks or months before I use a source again. Even if I remember the source, I may not remember the complete title, let alone the call number, and the library constantly rearranges the collection, so the source won't always be in the same place as when I last used it.

—Marcia Wyett, CGRS

Tip

PHOTOCOPYING TITLE PAGES

I make a photocopy of the title pages of new sources, making sure all the needed information for a complete source citation is listed. I also write the call number on the copy. I keep these copies in file folders labeled with the name of the repository where the source is located. Then when I am researching at that repository, I can take the file folder with me. I also check the file folder before I leave home to help plan my research trip to that facility.

Having copies of the title pages of sources also helps when typing client reports because I have all of the information for a complete source citation. When writing reports, I explain for the client a little about the source. Since I use many of the same sources for several clients, I have created a computer disk with these explanations and source citations. As I write the report, I can copy and paste this information into the report. This way, each report is specific to the client but not overly time consuming.

—Marcia Wyett, CGRS

---

then paste them into the report rather than retyping them over and over again. Also consider using a laptop for all of your client research and reports. Report writing is the part some genealogists like the least, so if you write the report as you are researching you will reduce the unpleasantness and be able to see holes in the research while you're still at the research facility.

While each professional has a personal style for report writing, here are the key elements of all reports, generally organized in this order:

- your name and address (if not using letterhead)
- client's name and address
- date of the report
- restatement of the client's research goal/request and time limitations
- summary of previous research (received from the client or based on your last report)
- discussion of repositories visited and new sources checked (e.g., limitations and idiosyncrasies of records, a repository's holdings, positive and negative research results with full source citations, etc.)
- analysis of research findings
- photocopies and/or abstracts of records with complete source citations (number each for easy referencing within the text of your report)
- suggestions for further research, which becomes your plan for the next phase of research

DAY PLANNER OR TICKLER FILE?

I attended a CareerTrack seminar on "How to Organize Your Life and Get Rid of Clutter." One of the tips I liked was the creation and use of a tickler file. (I guess it's supposed to tickle your brain into action.) This file should be in a convenient file drawer or, better yet, in a file crate, out in the open, with easy access. **Here's how it works:**

- Use forty-three hanging file folders to start the file.
- Label thirty-one of them 1 through 31; label the other twelve for the twelve months.
- Put the current month first, followed by the 1–31 folders.
- File notes and things that require action on a particular day of the current month, such as a note to make plane reservations or to mail in a conference registration. You can also include notes for deadlines to mail in handouts for lectures, deadlines for reports to clients, or when to bill clients.
- Anything beyond the current month gets placed into the appropriate month's folder. These items will be moved to the appropriate day folder on the first of that month when you rotate that month's folder forward. Or, when you have finished with 10 June, for example, it can become 10 July.
- When you start your day, review the contents of that day's folder, and take action on the items.
- Place that day's folder behind the last numbered folder for the next month.

This is essentially a day planner in file folder form, which may work better for you than a calendar or traditional day planner. While I like the tickler file idea, I don't have a space for another crate in my office or a drawer in which to put it.

Other Options

Some professionals keep track of their research time for clients in a day planner, others use a form they've designed, while others simply write their start and stop times at the top of their notes. I've tried all three and prefer the latter. I don't need to remember to bring along a day planner or a special form, and I need only look at my notes to find the times I worked for a particular client.

I also use a twelve-month-at-a-glance wall calendar since I like to see what's going on in my life for a whole year. On it I record deadlines in red, speaking engagements in green and beginning dates for writing and editing projects in blue. Since I lack wall space because of my floor-to-ceiling bookshelves, windows and computer desk hutch, the calendar hangs on a wall behind my office door. So I can see the calendar, I must close the door when I'm working. I generally do anyway to reduce unnecessary visits from those who also occupy my house and forget that I am working (of course, I do let the cats in). I also keep a duplicate in the form of a pocket calendar/address book to take with me when I travel.

CLIENT BILLING

Part of every professional genealogist's time is taken up with bookkeeping. Some genealogists prefer to bill clients on a case-by-case basis, while others pick a certain time of the month and bill them all. Using a computer to manage your accounts and do billing is probably the easiest and least time-consuming method.

When you bill clients, keep a hard copy of each statement in the separate billing file you have established for each client. Keep only these outstanding client files in a file holder on your desk. This way you can quickly see from which clients you have not yet received a payment and for whom you will not do any more work until the account has been paid.

Another method is to have a separate binder in which you keep all outstanding statements. The binder takes up less space on your desk than a file holder, but you will need to flip through the binder to see which clients owe you money or flag their statement with a self-stick note.

CERTIFICATION PROJECTS

See Also

Established in 1964, the Board for Certification of Genealogists (BCG) in Washington, DC, promotes excellence in genealogical research and writing. Genealogists may apply for certification in one of six categories and must pass the requirements of the chosen category. The two most popular are CGRS (Certified Genealogical Record Specialist) and CG (Certified Genealogist), so I will limit the discussion to organizing the requirements for these two projects **(see addresses, page 127). Organizing lineage society applications was covered in chapter six,** but not necessarily with the goal of submitting examples of your work for certification. Also keep in mind that the organizational method for certification could work just as easily if you are thinking of applying for accreditation through the Accredited Genealogists program in Salt Lake City, Utah (see addresses).

For both CG and CGRS projects, use a binder with subject dividers or use several file folders, whichever makes you comfortable. Label the subject dividers or folders for the requirements common to both and file relevant items accordingly:

- education and activities
- publications
- purpose of certification
- intended specialization
- accessibility of records
- reading and interpretation of documents
- use and interpretation of secondary sources

Then you will need folders or dividers for the additional specific requirements of the category you have selected:

For CGRS:
- three client reports (three folders)

For CG:
- three- to four-generation compiled genealogy (explained in more detail below)
- essay illustrating "genealogical proof standard" (formerly preponderance of evidence)
- one client report

While all the prerequisites require organization—in gathering and presenting the material—the three- to four-generation compiled genealogy is the one that is a major project, needing special attention. This project can feel overwhelming when you start: There is so much that you need to gather and on so many families. As with any other big project, break it down into manageable chunks by focusing on one family group at a time.

If you are using the surname/record type filing system, you may want to create temporary files just for this project, one per family group, to store acquired documents. If you are using the couple/family group filing system you're already set to go. Put the project files into a small file box or crate used specifically for this project. No doubt you will have documents that pertain to more than one family group and surname, such as photocopied pages from a cemetery transcription. In this case, you may want to also have a file folder for the locality, placing these types of records in it.

Begin writing the compiled genealogy as genealogical summaries (see chapter six) as soon as you decide upon a family. Once again, this is the best way to see holes in your research. You can use a to-do list specifically for this project, or you can write notes to yourself in the draft of the compilation, making the notations boldfaced and in brackets:

> In 1860, Archelus Marshall was farming in Orange County, Virginia. He was not reported as owning any real estate, but his personal property was valued at $4,438. He continued to farm in Orange County after the war, but he still did not own any property other than personal, which was valued at $700. [check slave schedules for 1860] By 1880, the family had moved to Spotsylvania County, where Archelus continued to farm.

Whether you use a color printer or not, today's word processing programs will allow you to use a color, such as red or blue, to highlight your notations or text so they will immediately come to your attention on the computer screen. As you conduct research, update your compilation and put a revision date on the first page.

The BCG will expect you to use one of the two standard numberings systems, either the Register System or the NGSQ System. These are descendancy number systems, which assign number 1 to the first person discussed in the genealogy. Here are extremely simplified versions of how both systems work.

Register System

1. Samuel^1 Ashton
    2.   i. Samuel^2 Ashton
    3. ii. Francis Ashton
       iii. Elizabeth Ashton

2. Samuel^2 Ashton (Samuel^1)
    4.   i. William^3 Ashton
       ii. Robert Ashton
    5. iii. Mary Ashton
    6. iv. Catlett Ashton

3. Francis^2 Ashton (Samuel^1)
    7.   i. Samuel^3 Ashton
    8. ii. George Ashton
    9. iii. Edward Ashton

4. William^3 Ashton (Samuel^2, Samuel^1)

- The superscript numbers after the first names of individuals are the generation numbers. Samuel is generation one; Samuel Jr. and Francis are generation two; William and Samuel III are generation three.
- The identifying numbers are the Arabic numerals. These are assigned to only those individuals who will be carried forward in the genealogy; in other words, the people assigned identifying numbers eventually married and had children. In this example, 2. Samuel, 3. Francis, 4. William, 5. Mary, 6. Catlett, 7. Samuel, 8. George and 9. Edward are all going to appear later in the genealogy as heads of households with families of their own. There will not be any further information written about Elizabeth and Robert Ashton.
- Lowercase Roman numerals indicate birth order and total number of children.

The problem with the Register System is if you discover information later about Elizabeth or Robert Ashton, you will have to renumber the entire genealogy. If you are using a computer genealogy software program that uses the Register System, however, it will automatically renumber for you.

NGSQ System

The NGSQ System is a modified version of the Register System; in fact you may hear it referred to as the Modified Register System. It works on the same premise.

1. Samuel^1 Ashton
 +2.   i. Samuel^2 Ashton
 +3. ii. Francis Ashton
  4. iii. Elizabeth Ashton

2. Samuel^2 Ashton (Samuel^1)
 +5.   i. William^3 Ashton
  6. ii. Robert Ashton
 +7. iii. Mary Ashton
 +8. iv. Catlett Ashton

- The superscript numbers after the first names of individuals are the generation numbers. They are set in italic, however, so they are not confused with footnote numbers.
- The identifying numbers are the Arabic numerals. Whereas the Register System assigns a number only to those individuals who will be carried forward in the genealogy, the NGSQ System gives everyone a number. To indicate a person is carried forward in the genealogy, a plus sign is placed

3. Francis² Ashton (Samuel¹)
+ 9.   i. Samuel³ Ashton
+10. ii. George Ashton
+11. iii. Edward Ashton

5. William³ Ashton (Samuel², Samuel¹)

before the number. This way, if more information is discovered on Elizabeth or Robert, you will not have to renumber. You would have to renumber if you discover another child and need to add that person to a family. Here again, if you are using a genealogy software program that uses the NGSQ System, it will automatically renumber for you.

• Lowercase Roman numerals indicate birth order and total number of children.

Consult Joan F. Curran's "Numbering Your Genealogy: Sound and Simple Systems,"in the September 1991 *National Genealogical Society Quarterly* (see bibliography on page 130), for a thorough explanation.

While no numbering system is 100 percent perfect, **use of other numbering systems, such as the so-called modern Henry System (which is actually older than the Register System and NGSQ System) or one you've invented, are not acceptable in a certification project.** Here's how the Henry System is supposed to work.

Warning

Henry System

1. Samuel Ashton
    11. Samuel Ashton
    12. Francis Ashton
    13. Elizabeth Ashton

11. Samuel Ashton
    111. William Ashton
    112. Robert Ashton
    113. Mary Ashton
    114. Catlett Ashton

12. Francis Ashton
    121. Samuel Ashton
    122. George Ashton
    123. Edward Ashton

Each child is first given the parent's ID number as a prefix to the birth order number. So the first child of number 1 is 11 (one, one; not eleven). The big problem here arises if there are more than nine children. Child number 10 of parent number 1 would have an identifying number of 110 and child number 11 would be 111, which throws off the numbering in the next generation. Another problem is the rapid increase in numbers. By the tenth generation, a person has more than ten identifying numbers. Do you want to try and figure out the ancestry of number 1673129462?

In an article for a genealogical magazine, I tried to point out that using a standard numbering system, such as the NGSQ System or the Register System, allows any genealogist to pick up a family history and immediately follow the descent. One does not have to wade through an explanation of a bizarre system to find who is related to whom and how the descendancy is followed. I was accused in a letter to the editor in the next issue, however, of bringing "to mind a witch doctor, dancing around a smoking fire shaking a gourd full of pebbles, feeding her patient lizard tongues and bat blood." (Okay, who's the smart aleck who told what I've been doing in my spare time?) The writer, who was attempting to praise the merits of the "refined, useful, modern . . . Henry System" continued, "Hopefully, we have all learned lizard tongues and bat blood are not the best medicine, and neither are the Register and NGSQ the best descendancy number systems, venerable though they may be."

Important

Regardless of whether you think the NGSQ and Register systems are the best ones, if you want to be certified and if you want to have your work understandable to all genealogists, you'll use one of them, which the major genealogical journals use. You would think that if the Henry System or some other numbering system were all that great, at least one of the respected genealogical journals would use it—but none do—or the BCG would allow you to use it—but it doesn't.

Organizing Your Certification Materials for Submission

Gale Williams Bamman wrote an excellent article for the May 1997 issue of the BCG newsletter *On Board*, which goes into more detail on how to organize your certification application. Here are the basics:

- Think of your application as a portfolio of your work.
- Use a lightweight, flexible-cover, three-ring binder for your portfolio. You can also use accordion files with labeled sections or labeled pocket folders. Remember, the weight limit is two pounds.
- Arrange your materials in the order in which they are requested in the application guide.
- Use subject dividers and label them with the item numbers or names of items.
- Have a separate section for those items retained in the BCG's files: final application form, signed Genealogist's Code and any cover letters you might include.

Organizing Your Recertification Materials

As soon as you get the happy news that you have become certified, start a folder for your recertification, which comes in five years. Make copies of your evaluations and put them in the recertification folder. You'll want to review these before you recertify to make sure you have addressed any weak areas the judges noted in the previous application. Place in the file items you might submit when you recertify: examples of outstanding client reports, articles you've written, etc. Start a list of your activities in the field (classes taught, publications, continuing education). As you update the list, keep it in your file. When the five years is up, you won't have to spend weeks compiling your recertification portfolio.

GENEALOGICAL INSTRUCTORS' AND SPEAKERS' LESSONS AND OVERHEADS

While there are certification categories for genealogical instructors and lecturers, the focus of this section is to help you organize your working materials. These tips could certainly apply to organizing the materials for certification as well.

Instructors may find it easiest to use a binder and corresponding subject dividers to hold lesson plans, handout masters and overheads. Keep overheads in top loading vinyl sheet protectors so you can easily put them on the overhead projector and avoid the static cling when two overheads are stored together.

Another method is to have a separate folder for each lesson, keeping the lecture, master handouts and relevant overheads together. This method keeps you from having to carry around your entire class curriculum every time you teach.

Lecturers can also use either binders or file folders for each lecture and its accompanying overhead transparencies. You can also handle overheads by purchasing cardboard frames for them, keeping the overheads and the lecture in the box in which the frames were bought. These boxes can easily be stored on your bookshelf and labeled on the spine. The main drawback to the frames and boxes is they are heavy and bulky to travel with.

If you are using slides, buy a carousel tray for each lecture; if the number of slides is small, then use one tray for two or more lectures. Store the carousel trays in the original boxes and label the boxes. Put these on your bookshelf. You can either put the lecture in a top loading file jacket on the shelf next to the slide box or in a folder in your filing cabinet.

Always keep a backup copy of your lecture at home if you are traveling. If you lose your lecture, someone at home can fax you a copy. Never let your lectures and overheads out of sight. Instead of packing them in checked baggage, take them in your carry-on bag. Remember, the show must go on. You can always buy a new outfit to lecture in if your suitcase visits Tahiti while you're in Idaho, but there's no presentation if you don't have your lectures and overheads.

ORGANIZATION AND TIME MANAGEMENT FOR GENEALOGICAL SPEAKERS

After you've been on the speaking circuit a few years, you may start to get more and more speaking engagements from genealogical societies around

Tip

ORGANIZING SLIDES FOR LECTURES

All slides for my lectures are kept in plastic slide boxes with the name of the lecture written on the outside. Each slide is numbered in the upper right corner by the way they fit into the carousel. That way they don't get out of order or upside down. I always do a quick runthrough before leaving for the lecture, but rarely do I have one in there incorrectly.

—Marsha Hoffman Rising, CG, FASG

Date	Society and Place	Honorarium	Handouts due	Plane Reserv.	Lectures
16 Aug 1998	Western Reserve Historical Society Cleveland, OH	$xxx	✓1 July 1998	I make ✓ done	1. From Italy to America 2. Italian-American Character 3. Immigrant Experience
18–22 Aug 1998	FGS Conference Cincinnati	$xxx	✓1 April 1998	I make ✓ done	1. Love Letters 2. Immigrant Experience 3. From Italy to America 4. Career Options

the country. Many societies will write to inquire about your fees and topics, giving you the date of their seminar to see if you are available. Always check your calendar before you respond. Though that may seem obvious, more than one speaker has accidentally booked two engagements for the same day. It's also a wise idea to let the inquiring society know that you will only hold the date open for that group for thirty days without a confirmation from them. I have had on a couple of occasions two groups that want me for the same date. I let the second group know that if I do not hear back from the first group within thirty days, then they can have the date.

Start a file folder labeled "Potential Speaking Engagements" or "Speaking Inquiries" to keep copies of all letters written to you and your responses. If the society does engage your services, start a separate file folder for each engagement, and keep copies of all communications with the society in it, including your contract or terms of agreement. When you get your airline tickets, put those in the folder, too. Also keep a copy of the handouts you send.

When you start getting several speaking engagements a year, you may want to create a list, like the one shown above, to post in your office or work area to remind you of deadlines and various details about the engagement: when to have masters of your handouts in, how much you'll be paid, whether you or the society need to make your plane reservations and what lectures you are to present. Place a check mark by each item when you complete it.

If you are creating new lectures, you need to allow several weeks before your speaking engagement to write the lecture and create visual aids. Don't forget, this is not counting time to research the lecture material! Even if it is a lecture you've presented a zillion times, you still need to look it over in plenty of time to make any revisions and updates.

THE ACTIVE PROFESSIONAL

Most professionals are busy not only with their client work, but they also do public speaking, teach classes, do volunteer work for genealogical societies and write articles and books. Keeping on top of all these activities requires refined organizational skills. You cannot survive as a professional without them. You will definitely need your own private work space, and you will require undisturbed space to put the tools of your trade. If you haven't yet hung out your shingle, make sure you consider all these aspects.

TEN

Organizing and Preserving Your Genealogy for the Future

E very genealogist's worst nightmare is having descendants destroy practically a lifetime of genealogical research after the genealogist is dead and gone. Every descendant's worst nightmare is having to sort through practically a lifetime of genealogical research after the genealogist is dead and gone. Surely there is a way we genealogists can avoid these horrifying dreams for both parties. The solution is to be organized and prepared for the inevitable.

The obsessive-compulsive organized genealogist will routinely purge files and reduce the amount of genealogical clutter, making the descendants' lives easier. But what about the rest of us who are moderately organized? Is our stuff doomed? Not if we take at least a few precautions.

PROVIDING FOR THE FUTURE

One of the easy methods to ensure your genealogy survives is to make a provision for it in your will. Bequeath the material to a trusted descendant who will treasure your research efforts as much as you do. If there are no trustworthy descendants to whom you feel comfortable leaving your genealogy, then make provisions to have it donated to a genealogical library or archive. Always check with the facility first to see if they can accommodate your materials. Include instructions allowing a genealogy buddy to sort through your materials, determining what can be pitched and what can't. Even if you are leaving your materials to a repository, someone will have to weed through your papers and decide what should be kept. You cannot realistically expect anyone to take everything you have collected and keep it intact.

If there are materials you feel strongly about preserving, include them in your will or your instructions. In my case, I would come back to haunt the person who destroys or pitches my diaries, which I have kept since I was

Idea Generator

115

For More Info

FOR MORE EXCERPTS

For more excerpts of the diary, see *Revelations: Diaries of Women*, edited by Mary Jane Moffat and Charlotte Painter (New York: Vintage Books, 1974), 14.

ten. I share Marie Bashkirtseff's (1860–1884) feelings. She wrote in her diary:

> What if, seized without warning by a fatal illness, I should happen to die suddenly! . . . And after my death they would rummage among my papers; they would find my journal, and destroy it after having read it, and soon nothing would be left of me—nothing—nothing—nothing! This is the thought that has always terrified me.

So I have left written instructions in the fire-safe filing box that contains my diaries that my daughter is to inherit them, and they are to be treated as the family jewels, passed down from one generation to the next (this is also a provision in my will). If no one in the family wants them, then they are to be donated to a local historical society or library with a special collections department. Another provision is they are not to be published until after the fiftieth anniversary of my death. Even if I were to die tomorrow, presumably all the guilty parties I've named as partners in crime would be dead fifty years later.

NATURAL AND UNNATURAL DISASTERS

Important

Not only must you think about the future of your genealogical materials in the hands of your descendants, but you must also consider what would happen if your home met with a disaster: fire, flood, hurricane, tornado, vandalism, theft. This is a devastating thought for anyone, genealogist or not. It may take another lifetime to reconstruct what you've collected thus far, but how long would it take you to get somewhat operational again? From memory, could you make a list of documents you know you have collected? Could you reconstruct your pedigree chart from memory—maybe not the dates, but at least the names? Give serious thought to what you need to safeguard and how you will ensure its safety.

FIRE-SAFE FILING BOXES AND SAFE-DEPOSIT BOXES

To protect those items you would absolutely hate to lose in the event of a fire, invest in a couple of fire-safe filing boxes or a fire-safe filing cabinet. Most fire-safe boxes ensure the safety of paper items, which char at 450°F. Media such as computer disks, audiotapes and videotapes, and photographic film and negatives are in danger if temperatures merely reach 125°F. During a typical house fire, temperatures begin at 350°F but can rise to 2000°F during a flash fire. Before you purchase a fire-safe file cabinet or chest, think about what you want to protect, then make sure you are purchasing the right product. There are special containers specifically for media storage.

You cannot ensure the safety of all of your genealogical materials and heirlooms, so you will need to make some tough decisions on what will go in fire-safe containers. After my diaries, my next irreplaceable items are family photographs. Since it would be impossible to save them all, I have made copies of the ones for which I do not have negatives. Rather than keeping the photographs in the fire-safe file box, I keep the negatives there. Making sure relatives have copies of the more important family pictures is another way of ensuring their safety. (More information on preserving and organizing photographs appears on page 119.) Another alternative is to rent a safe-deposit box at your local bank and store family artifacts in it.

DONATING OR PUBLISHING CHUNKS OF RESEARCH

If I were to lose every bit of research I have gathered on my Ebetino family, I would not be too heartbroken. Why? Because I have published a book on that family and donated it to various libraries across the country. It is also available on microfilm through the Family History Library in Salt Lake City. If I were to lose every bit of research I have gathered on my Fitzhugh family, I would be heartsick; I have not yet published it. I could reconstruct it, but it would take years.

Publishing chunks of your research is one way to ensure that nothing will ever happen to it. If your descendants come along and throw away all of your files, charts and forms, or if they aren't aware that the data is on your computer, the information will still be preserved for all time if you have published it in some form (book, article, manuscript or as part of a computer database).

Idea Generator

When I say "publish," I do not necessarily mean writing a formal book, elegantly bound by a printer, which you sell to relatives, although that is certainly the ultimate way to preserve your research. I'm talking distribution. Compile and document your genealogy, make several copies, distribute it to relatives, but more important, send copies to a few libraries across the country, such as the Family History Library in Salt Lake City and libraries or historical societies for the areas in which your ancestors lived. If you send it to the Family History Library, include permission for the manuscript to be microfilmed. Once it is on microfilm, a copy will be kept in their climate-controlled, mountainside vault for all eternity. You couldn't ask for better than that. The Family History Library will also accept your genealogy on computer disk to include in their Ancestral File. At the Family History Library in Salt Lake City or at one of its worldwide Family History Centers, ask for the leaflet "Contributing Information on Ancestral File."

You do not have to have your genealogy finished to distribute it. You can always do revised editions or supplements, no matter which form you have made it available in. To make it easier on yourself and those receiving copies, donate chunks of research at a time. Analyze your charts and forms to determine for which families you have a significant amount of research, then prepare it in a format to distribute.

Naturally, when you distribute your genealogy—regardless of the format—it needs to be organized and fully documented for another person to get full use from the data (and isn't that the point of doing your genealogy in the first place?). Your research needs to be prepared in a standard genealogical format using a standard genealogical numbering system. Consult the references in the bibliography on page 130 for help in this area.

PRESERVING ORIGINAL DOCUMENTS

Warning

Sources

The fortunate genealogist has inherited original documents: letters, diaries, private and public documents. Avoid working with the originals, and if you must, wear cotton gloves. It is preferable to make photocopies to work with. Put the original documents in an appropriate type of archival-quality container—folders, boxes, bags—and store them in a bank safe-deposit box.

Archival-quality products can be purchased from mail-order companies that specialize in these items **(see addresses, page 127). Also check with a local museum.** They may sell archival-quality products in their gift shop, or they may be willing to share an order, since it is often cheaper to buy these items in bulk. Also ask the museum curator for advice on restoration and preservation for specific items.

You might also want to consider donating original documents now, keeping photocopies for yourself and interested family members. A museum or archive will take the proper measures to preserve these valuable items.

FAMILY ALBUMS AND SCRAPBOOKS

Another method of organizing and preserving your family history is to make family albums or scrapbooks out of your research for your descendants.

Tip

PRESENTATION OF RESEARCH RESULTS AND DOCUMENTS

Some of my clients want to give their parents or children a gift of genealogical research, so I've developed a package that organizes research results and documents. I purchase an archival heritage album (with slipcase) and place all the documents and reports in Poly-vu sheets. At the beginning of the album is a computerized pedigree chart, followed by tabs for each ancestor. The first page for each ancestor is a computerized family group sheet, followed by documents for that person in chronological order. For example, after the family group sheet you may find a census enumeration, marriage record, land deeds, military pension, obituary and will. Maps and photographs of the family are merged into the total package.

—Kathleen W. Hinckley, CGRS

You can do an album (archival-quality binder) for each surname, taking the ancestral line back as far as possible. Along with pedigree charts and family group sheets, you can add photographs and documents you have collected. Place the items in top loading, acid-free sheet protectors. These items may be purchased through an archival supply catalog, some office supply stores and some nationwide hobby stores.

You can organize the album any way you want, but most common is to start with the present and work backward. For example, if the album is on your paternal line, begin with a family group sheet for you, your spouse and your family, then photographs and documents pertaining to them. Follow this with a group sheet and materials for your parents, then your paternal grandparents, and so forth. Or you can organize an album for your "umbilical" or maternal line: you, your mom, your mom's mom (maternal grandmother), your mom's maternal grandmother, and so on. Use divider tabs for each new family group. You may also want to include a computer-generated chart to show relationships and ancestry.

The Problems of a Unique Album

There is one major problem with doing a family album: Usually there is only one copy. Making additional copies for family members would be ideal, but they are costly to make if you are using archival-quality products to ensure the album and its contents will be around for generations to come. The distribution will also be limited. This would not be something you would donate to libraries for their collections. This is an item that is destined to end up in an antique store if a descendant does not realize its value. Antique stores typically remove the old photographs to sell separately and toss anything strangers would not buy.

If you make only one album, make absolutely sure it is included in your will and you think carefully about the person to whom you will leave it. This is a one-of-a-kind item, and you want to stress its importance and heirloom quality.

Besides making albums or scrapbooks of your family history, don't forget yourself! If you have items that hold special memories for you—ribbons, photographs, newspaper clippings, pressed flowers—put them in an album or scrapbook. Consolidating these items immediately conveys that they were special. To ensure that descendants know the value these mementos have for you, write a short piece explaining why each item is so important and keep it in the scrapbook next to the item.

ORGANIZING AND PRESERVING PHOTOGRAPHS

You need to take some measures to ensure the family photographs will be around for generations to enjoy. Make copies of rare photographs (i.e., those without a negative) as soon as possible. Should something happen to the original, having a negative is just as important as having a positive copy. Photography stores can make "copy negs," but this can get costly if you

Tip

STORING FOREIGN DOCUMENTS

I place foreign documents/ photocopies in an archival-quality sheet saver and type a translation of the document, which is slipped into the other side of the sleeve. This will ensure that people who can't read the language will know what it is about, and it saves me time, too. When I am doing more research, I have a quick English translation.

—Regina Hines Ellison, CGRS

Reminder

Tip

ORGANIZING YOUR OLD PHOTOGRAPHS

One of the easiest methods for organizing your original family photographs is to group them by size. This can be done by purchasing archival-quality plastic sheets that have pockets in them. These come in many different sizes to accommodate almost any popular size original, even if they were mounted on a mount board.

If you would prefer to organize them by date, you would need several extra pocket sleeves because each decade of photographs had various sizes that were popular at certain times. Therefore, you may have one page containing one or two 5″×7″ photographs from the 1880s, for example, and another page containing one or two 8″×10″ photographs from the 1890s.

Other options are to use archival photo albums with archival pages, using archival corner mounts. This would enable you to display several photographs of various sizes on a single page, but such albums are usually quite expensive because of the high-quality materials used.

If you have any copy negatives, these same pages also come in sizes that can store negatives of various sizes. Never store the negatives with the prints. One of the best places to store your negatives or originals is in a safe-deposit box in a local bank. The temperature, humidity and darkness are ideal for preservation purposes.

—David L. Mishkin, President, Just Black & White

have several done. You can make copies and negatives yourself by simply photographing a photograph.

Use a 35mm camera with a focusable lens. Magnifying lenses can be added, so you can fill the entire frame with the photo if it is a small one. After you develop the film, this gives you a negative of the photograph. Black-and-white film and negatives will last longer than color, but if the photograph is sepia toned or has been colored, you will lose that quality with black-and-white film. The solution is to make copies using both color and black-and-white film.

Though it won't give you a negative, you can copy photographs on color photocopy machines, or you can scan photographs into your computer using a scanner. Be careful of exposing old photographs to the intense light used by photocopiers and scanners. Repeated exposure can damage the photograph. Another possibility is to use a digital camera to make copies of your photographs, which you can then store on your computer or on a disk. Remember, however, we don't yet know the true life of computer disk and hardware storage. Since we cannot possibly know the technology of the future, there is

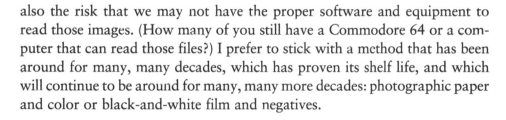

ORGANIZING YOUR NEW PHOTOGRAPHS

Most family photographs taken today are in color. Most people are not aware that color photographs (especially those that are displayed) will not last more than fifty years. Keeping that in mind, one of the best ways to organize the photos you take today is to store them in archival pocket sleeves as you would the older photographs.

Most photographs you get today are either 3½"×5" or 4"×6". The plastic pocket sleeves are available in both sizes. Many manufacturers of these sleeves also have areas on each sheet where you can record the event, people and places photographed. Do this for future generations so they won't have the same problems you are encountering with old photographs.

Photographs can be organized into three-ring binders and each book could cover a time period, individual, event or location (such as a vacation). Organize negatives in the same way.

—David L. Mishkin, President, Just Black & White

also the risk that we may not have the proper software and equipment to read those images. (How many of you still have a Commodore 64 or a computer that can read those files?) I prefer to stick with a method that has been around for many, many decades, which has proven its shelf life, and which will continue to be around for many, many more decades: photographic paper and color or black-and-white film and negatives.

Identifying Photographs

Of course, we have all been frustrated when confronted with unidentified photographs. Don't make the same mistake your ancestors and relatives did. Always identify the people, place and date of a photograph whenever possible. After you've made copies of photographs, circulate the copies among family members to see if they can identify the people, events and dates of the photos. **Also use books such as Thomas L. Davies's *Shoots: A Guide to Your Family's Photographic Heritage* and Joan Severa's *Dressed for the Photographer: Ordinary Americans and Fashion, 1840–1900*,** which will help you identify the time period based on the type of photograph, poses and clothing. But do not write the information on the fronts or backs of photographs. Ink may bleed through to the front, and pencil causes indentations on the photograph. You can use labels, writing on the label then affixing it to the photograph, but it is best to use archival-quality labels. These have special adhesive that is not harmful to the photograph. Plus, the adhesive on regular labels usually wears off after awhile, so the label no longer sticks.

One method of marking photographs, while preserving the original, is to

For More Info

use an archival-quality pen and lightly put a number in a corner on the back. Then make a corresponding list with identifying information. Put the photos in archival-quality sheet protectors, then place them in a binder with the list. I would be worried, however, that the list would get separated from the photographs. Another solution is to buy special sheet protectors, allowing you to either write on the sheet protector or to include a descriptive note about each photo in special sleeves.

Sources

Sheet protectors and storage boxes for photographs, negatives and slides, as well as archival-quality binders, can be purchased through mail-order catalogs. It is sometimes cheaper to buy these items in bulk, so perhaps a friend would want to split the cost. **See addresses, page 127**, for a list of some archival and preservation suppliers. Some of the large hobby store chains are starting to carry archival-quality materials and at less cost, so check these places, too.

The arrangement of photographs within an album is your personal preference. You can arrange them by generation, family members, time period, photo size. Put a cover sheet in the album to explain your system, so when someone takes over this project, they will be consistent. By the same token, if you are the recipient of a photo album, do not disturb the arrangement of the original. If you need to replace the album, especially if it is one of those with "magnetic" pages, keep the photos in the original order when you transfer them to a new album.

OTHER FAMILY ARTIFACTS

For More Info

The archival and preservation suppliers listed in the addresses on page 127 also sell boxes and storage containers for other treasured family artifacts, whether they are historical documents or material items such as quilts, jewelry or silverware. Make sure you label or identify items you want your descendants to preserve and create an inventory of them. Then, store or display them. **Russell D. Earnest, in *Grandma's Attic: Making Heirlooms Part of Your Family History*, discusses ways to set up a family museum with family artifacts, as well as other aspects you need to consider:** researching and interpreting artifacts, preserving heirlooms, acquiring appraisals and insurance, and creating and adding heirlooms from your generation.

If you have original historical documents—papers, letters, diaries and so forth—make photocopies for your files and work with these. Store and preserve the originals in archival-quality containers or donate them now to places where they will be preserved. This would also apply to items you may have from your own lifetime that you wish to be saved for future generations to enjoy.

As Earnest explains in *Grandma's Attic*, think of yourself as the curator or caretaker of the family's history and heirlooms. That's a big responsibility and one I'm sure you don't take lightly. It's up to you to maintain your genealogy and historical artifacts in good condition and to protect them from loss or destruction.

PRESERVING FAMILY PAPERS

My husband's grandfather Frank Sturdevant (1889–1950) was a lifelong family historian. He collected enough information and memorabilia to fill many large boxes, but he never organized it all, nor did he ever write or chart the entire family history the way he always intended to do. He frequently wrote genealogical information on small slips of paper or the backs of envelopes, usually without source citations. As we transcribe and organize what he left, we would not toss his original notes. Being from Frank, in his own hand, based on his familiarity with everyone from his Civil War grandfather to cousins he visited across the country before World War I, each note is already an heirloom. Yet I was unsure how to cite his scraps. Finally, I decided to declare everything the "Frank Sturdevant Papers," as in an archive, and to cite and explain that as a source. I am using archival methods to organize the papers, and they will eventually go to a historical society. Consider this approach to older family papers. There is a sense of pride and honor in finishing what a beloved ancestor set out to do.

—Katherine Scott Sturdevant, historian

By researching and recording the family stories and history of artifacts, you are making them even more valuable to future generations. Keep a copy of this research with the items, as well as in your files. You may also want to photograph items for your files, too. I don't know what will become of my great-grandmother's dishes—the ones she brought with her from Italy in 1910—when my first cousin, two generations removed, dies. She inherited the dishes and they sit in her china cabinet. She is unmarried and has no children. Although I have tried to impart to her the historical and familial value they have to me and future generations, I do not know to whom she will leave those dishes—a niece or nephew, perhaps—if anyone. But I do have a photograph of them.

Along with photographing artifacts and heirlooms known to be in the possession of your relatives, you may want to create an inventory of these items to keep in your files. The Artifacts and Heirlooms in Other People's Possession form (page 146) is one way to keep track of these. Besides recording information about the item and who currently owns it, you also want to record by whom that item is to be inherited. This forces your relatives to think about the item and a likely candidate who would equally value the heirloom.

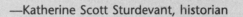

A Useful Form You Can Reproduce
For a full-sized blank copy of the Artifacts and Heirlooms in Other People's Possession form, see page 146. You are free to photocopy this form for personal use.

PUBLISHING ANCESTORS' LETTERS AND DIARIES

Along with photocopying and properly storing ancestors' letters and diaries you may have inherited, you may want to publish (or distribute) them.

For More Info

Tip

Working from photocopies of the documents, transcribe them fully as they were written. If you need to edit them for readability or want to annotate them with additional research, **consult a guide such as Katherine Scott Sturdevant's "Documentary Editing for Family Historians"** published in the *Association of Professional Genealogists Quarterly* or **Mary-Jo Kline's *A Guide to Documentary Editing* (see the bibliography on page 127)**. Transcriptions and especially annotated diaries and letters of ordinary people are material that university presses are inclined to publish. This is an excellent way of preserving and distributing a part of your family history at someone else's cost.

STORING DATA ON MICROFORM OR CD-ROM

If you are becoming overrun with paper and you live in fear that your house may one day spontaneously combust, consider transferring some of your data onto microfiche, microfilm or CD-ROM. Most major cities have businesses that offer data storage. Look in the yellow pages under "CD-ROM Services," "Data Storage," "Microfilm Storage" or "Office Records Stored." As with any other service or product, shop around and get prices for various storage media. Also consider having more than one copy made and storing it someplace other than your home.

Think about the future and how the stored item will be accessed. If you don't have a microfilm or microfiche reader, you will need to purchase one in order to view the data you've stored, or you will need to use a reader at a library. The Colorado State Archives offered to microfilm all the old issues of our local newspaper at no cost to the publisher and to provide them with duplicates of the microfilms. The only problem is the newspaper office does not have a microfilm reader to view the reels.

Storage Longevity

If you store data on a CD-ROM, can you feel confident that CD-ROM data will be accessible to people one hundred or more years from now? Technology changes awfully fast. Remember eight-track tapes? Reel-to-reel tapes? Beta videotapes? Do you still have machines that can play back these items?

Even the government is struggling with retrieving data stored on old computer tapes. The National Archives has many computerized records made just thirty years ago, such as census data from the 1960s, that cannot be read today. If you were computer savvy thirty years ago, you may also remember computer punch cards. Because the National Archives does not have the funds, staff or machines to retrieve the extensive records of Americans who served in World War II, researchers can only access the material through sixteen hundred reels of microfilm of the original computer punch cards. My suggestion is to go with a storage method that has proven itself over several decades and that will be with us for many, many more. Microfiche or microfilm has been in continual use for more than seventy years. The Family History Library in Salt Lake City has more than two million rolls of microfilm kept in a climate-controlled vault in the side of a mountain. No doubt they also have film readers there, too. The National Archives probably has just as many films. I think it's safe to say that microforms will be around for a long, long time.

According to an article in the 20 April 1998, issue of *Business Week*, "under less-than-optimal storage conditions, digital tapes and disks, including CD-ROMs and optical drives, might deteriorate about as fast as newsprint—in five to ten years." The National Media Lab has been running tests on various computer media. Under optimal conditions, it reports, a CD-ROM could last up to fifty years.

Though the quality and longevity of CD-ROMs is likely to improve over the next few years, can we be certain that we will have the computer software and hardware needed to read them in fifty to one hundred or more years?

You decide. Here are the projected life expectancies of various information storage media kept under proper climate-controlled conditions. The data is based on research conducted by the National Media Lab, *using the highest quality products available and optimal storage conditions*:

audiotapes and videotapes	10 years
newspaper	20 years
CD-ROM	50 years
archival-quality microfilm	200 years
archival-quality paper	500 years

Which media would you trust to preserve your family history?

Of course, if you really want to guarantee longevity, you'll ignore the above and transfer all of your data to stone. The Rosetta stone dates back to the reign of Ptolemy V before 180 B.C. Stone carvings in caves or pyramids seem to have the longest life of all media—just a thought.

THE BEST METHOD OF ENSURING YOUR RESEARCH IS HERE TO STAY

If you are thinking of publishing the results of your research, do it. I know it's a lot of work. But books have been around for centuries and are here to stay. Computer technology and the Internet will *never* replace books. Are you going to sit and read a five-hundred-page book from your computer monitor? No one will. Will you print it out to read? I doubt it. We like the feel of a book. We like the smell of the ink. We like to turn pages. It's portable. It's comfortable. It's familiar. We can read it anywhere, anytime. We don't even need electricity to read it. Sunlight or a candle will do. More than 62,000 titles were published in 1995—an all-time high for book publishing.

There is no doubt in my mind that the best and safest way to preserve your genealogy for the future is to publish it on quality paper, distribute it to several libraries and donate a copy to the Family History Library in Salt Lake City. Authorize its microfilming so a copy will be stored in their vault. There's no cost to you to have it put on microfilm and stored. It's that simple.

INCENTIVE FOR STAYING ORGANIZED

You may decide to use a combination of these methods to organize and preserve your family history for your descendants. It doesn't matter which one you choose. The important part is to seriously consider the destiny of your years of work and research and to prepare for it. Your research is your legacy to your family. By organizing it, keeping it organized and making it available to others, you can rest assured that it won't be lost or destroyed after you die.

You had no idea what you were getting yourself into when you decided genealogy would be a fun hobby or profession, did you? If reading this book has made you feel tired and overwhelmed and you haven't even begun to practice any of the ideas, then maybe you'll want to consider a different pastime. But if it has made you feel tired, overwhelmed and just a little bit inspired, stick with it. You won't find a more rewarding and enjoyable endeavor as researching your family history. Now, if you can just keep it all organized. . . .

Addresses

Sources

Genealogical Societies

Federation of Genealogical Societies
P.O. Box 200940, Austin, TX 78720-0940
phone: (888) 347-1500   *fax*: (512) 336-2732
E-mail: fgs-office@fgs.org   *Web site*: http://www.fgs.org
National Genealogical Society and National Genealogical
Society Computer Interest Group
4527 17th St., North, Arlington, VA 22207-2399
phone: (703) 525-0050 or (800) 473-0060   *fax*: (703) 525-0052
E-mail: 76702.2417@compuserve.com
Web site: http://www.genealogy.org/~ngs/
New England Historic Genealogical Society
99/101 Newbury St., Boston, MA 02116
phone: (617) 536-5740   *fax*: (617) 536-7307
E-mail: 74777.3612@compuserve.com
Web site: http://www.nehgs.org

Professional Organizations

Accredited Genealogists
Family History Library
35 North West Temple, Salt Lake City, UT 84150
Association of Professional Genealogists
P.O. Box 40393, Denver, CO 80204-0393
E-mail: apg-admin@apgen.org   *Web site*: http://www.apgen.org/~apg/
Board for Certification of Genealogists
P.O. Box 14291, Washington, DC 20044
Web site: http://www.genealogy.org/~bcg
Genealogical Speakers Guild
2818 Pennsylvania Ave. NW, Suite 159, Washington, DC 20007

Genealogical Supplies

(Books, Forms, Charts and Conference Tapes)
Ancestry Incorporated
P.O. Box 476, Salt Lake City, UT 84110
phone: (800) 262-3787   *fax*: (801) 426-3501
E-mail: info@ancestry.com   *Web site*: http://www.ancestry.com
Everton Publishers
P.O. Box 368, Logan, UT 84321
E-mail: catalog@everton.com   *Web site*: http://www.everton.com

Frontier Press
P.O. Box 126, Cooperstown, NY 13326
phone: (800) 772-7559 *fax*: (607) 547-9415
E-mail: kgfrontier@aol.com *Web site*: http://www.doit.com/frontier
Genealogical Publishing Co., Inc.
1001 N. Calvert St., Baltimore, MD 21202
phone: (800) 296-6687 *fax*: (410) 752-8492
Hearthstone Bookshop
5735-A Telegraph Rd., Alexandria, VA 22303
phone: (888) 960-3300 *fax*: (703) 960-0087
E-mail: info@hearthstonebooks.com
Web site: http://www.hearthstonebooks.com
Heritage Books
1540E Pointer Ridge Place, Suite 140, Bowie, MD 20716
phone: (800) 398-7709
National Archives Trust Fund
NEPS Dept. 735, P.O. Box 100793, Atlanta, GA 30384
E-mail: inquire@nara.gov *Web site*: http://www.nara.gov
Repeat Performance (national genealogical conference tapes)
2911 Crabapple Lane, Hobart, IN 46342
phone: (219) 465-1234

Genealogical Lending Libraries

Heritage Quest Genealogical Services (formerly American Genealogical Lending Library)
P.O. Box 329, Bountiful, UT 84011-0329
phone: (800) 760-2455 *fax*: (801) 298-5468
E-mail: sales@heritagequest.com
Web site: http://www.heritagequest.com
National Archives Microfilm Rental Program
P.O. Box 30, Annapolis Junction, MD 20701-0030
phone: (301) 604-3699
National Genealogical Society
(see address at page 127)
New England Historic Genealogical Society
(see address at page 127)

Genealogical Software

Brøderbund Software
Banner Blue Division
P.O. Box 6125, Novato, CA 94948-9825
phone: (800) 315-0669
Web site: http://www.familytreemaker.com
Brother's Keeper
John Steed
6907 Childsdale Ave., Rockford, MI 49341

phone: (616) 364-5503   *fax*: (616) 866-3345

E-mail: 75745.1371@compuserve.com

Web site: http://ourworld.compuserve.com/homepages/Brothers_Keeper

Family Gathering

   Commsoft, Inc.

   Palladium Interactive, Inc.

   P.O. Box 1200, Windsor, CA 95492

   phone: (707) 836-9000   *fax*: (707) 838-6343

   E-mail: familygathering@cmmsft.com

   Web site: http://www.palladiumnet.com/familygathering

Family Tree Maker

   (see Brøderbund Software listed above)

The Master Genealogist

   Wholly Genes Software

   5144 Flowertuft Ct., Columbia, MD 21075

   phone: (800) 982-2103   *E-mail*: tmg@whollygenes.com

   Web site: http://www.whollygenes.com

Personal Ancestral File

   Salt Lake Distribution Center

   1999 W. 1700 South, Salt Lake City, UT 84104

   phone: (800) 346-6044

Reunion

   Leister Productions

   P.O. Box 289, Mechanicsburg, PA 17055

   phone: (717) 697-1378   *fax*: (717) 697-4373

   E-mail: 7477.1626@compuserve.com

   Web site: http://www.leisterpro.com

Roots V

   Commsoft, Inc.

   P.O. Box 310, Windsor, CA 95492-0310

   phone: (800) 327-6687   *E-mail*: info@cmmsft.com

Sky Software

   (makers of Sky Index and Sky Filer)

   4675 York One Rd., Lineboro, MD 21102

   phone: (800) 776-0137   *fax*: (410) 374-3484

   Web site: http://www.sky-software.com

Ultimate Family Tree

   Palladium Interactive

   P.O. Box 6907, San Rafael, CA 94903-0907

   phone: (888) 891-1919   *fax*: (415) 446-1726

   E-mail: ultimatedata@palladium.net

   Web site: http://www.familyinfo.com

Archival and Preservation Suppliers

Light Impressions

   439 Monroe Ave., P.O. Box 940, Rochester, NY 14607-3717

phone: (800) 828-6216   *fax*: (800) 828-5539
Restoration Source
   P.O. Box 9384, Salt Lake City, UT 84109-0384
   phone: (801) 278-7880   *fax*: (801) 278-3015
University Products
   P.O. Box 101, South Canal St., Holyoke, MA 01041-0101
   phone: (800) 628-1912

Photograph Copying and Restoration Services
Copy and Restoration
   P.O. Box 7058, San Mateo, CA 94403
   phone: (800) 874-7327
Duplitech
   P.O. Box 4154, Salem, OR 97302
   phone: (503) 378-0751
Just Black & White
   P.O. Box 4628, 54 York St., Portland, ME 04112
   phone: (800) 827-5881

Printed Source

Bibliography

Anderson, Robert C., Sharon DeBartolo Carmack, and Marty Hiatt. "Professional Genealogists Offer Tips for 'Painlessly' Moving Your Office." *Association of Professional Genealogists Quarterly* 9 (June 1994): 36-38.

Aslett, Don. *Clutter Free! Finally and Forever*. Pocatello, Idaho: Marsh Creek Press, 1995.

———. *Clutter's Last Stand*. Cincinnati: Writer's Digest Books, 1984.

———. *How to Have a 48-Hour Day*. Pocatello, Idaho: Marsh Creek Press, 1996.

———. *The Office Clutter Cure*. Cincinnati: Betterway Books, 1994.

Bamman, Gale Williams. "Application Strategies: Organizing Your Materials." *On Board*, the newsletter of the Board for Certification of Genealogists, 3 (May 1997): 11-12.

———. "How a Laptop Can Save You Time and Your Client Money." *Association of Professional Genealogists Quarterly* 8 (September 1993): 59-60.

Boorstin, Daniel J. "I Cannot Live Without Books." *Parade Magazine* (12 July 1998): 12-13.

CareerTrack. *How to Organize Your Life and Get Rid of Clutter*. Boulder, CO: CareerTrack, 1995.

Carmack, Sharon DeBartolo. *The Genealogy Sourcebook*. Los Angeles: Lowell House, 1997.

————. "There's More Here Than Meets the Eye: A Closer Look at Cemetery Research and Transcribing Projects." Federation of Genealogical Societies' *FORUM* 7 (fall 1995): 1, 16-17.

————. "The Editor's Craft." Federation of Genealogical Societies' *FORUM* 8 (winter 1996): 22-23.

Chamberlin, David C. *The Conceptual Approach to Genealogy: Essential Methodology for Organizing and Compiling Genealogical Records.* Salt Lake City: Ancestry, Inc., 1998.

"Client Files: Responses to the Question of the Quarter." *Association of Professional Genealogists Quarterly* 10 (December 1995): 116-18.

Clifford, Karen. *Becoming an Accredited Genealogist: 100 Tips to Ensure Your Success.* Salt Lake City: Ancestry, Inc., 1998.

Croom, Emily Anne. *The Unpuzzling Your Past Workbook.* Cincinnati: Betterway Books, 1996.

Culp, Stephanie. *How to Get Organized When You Don't Have the Time.* Cincinnati: Writer's Digest Books, 1986.

Curran, Joan Ferris. "Numbering Your Genealogy: Sound and Simple Systems." *National Genealogical Society Quarterly* 79 (September 1991): 183-93.

Davies, Thomas L. *Shoots: A Guide to Your Family's Photographic Heritage.* Danbury, NH: Addison House, 1977.

Dollarhide, William. *Managing a Genealogical Project.* Baltimore: Genealogical Publishing Co., 1996.

Dorff, Pat. *File—Don't Pile! For People Who Write.* New York: St. Martin's Press, 1994.

Earnest, Russell D. *Grandma's Attic: Making Heirlooms Part of Your Family History.* Albuquerque, NM: Russell D. Earnest Associates, 1991.

Everton, George B., comp. *The Handy Book for Genealogists*, 8th ed. Logan, Utah: Everton Publishers, 1991.

Eichholz, Alice. *Ancestry's Red Book: American State, County, and Town Sources*, rev. ed. Salt Lake City: Ancestry, Inc., 1992.

Geiger, Linda A. Woodward. "Techniques for Transcribing and Abstracting Documents." *Association of Professional Genealogists Quarterly* 10 (September 1995): 87-88.

Hatcher, Patricia Law. *Producing a Quality Family History.* Salt Lake City: Ancestry, Inc., 1996.

Hatcher, Patricia Law, and John V. Wylie. *Indexing Family Histories.* Arlington, VA: National Genealogical Society Special Publication, 1994.

Hemphill, Barbara. *Taming the Paper Tiger: Organizing the Paper in Your Life*, 4th ed. New York: Times Business Books, 1997.

"Historic Catch-22: As Computers Got Better, Early Data Now Unreadable." Washington, DC: Association Press, 2 January 1991. Reprinted in *Association of Professional Genealogists Quarterly* 6 (fall 1991): 61.

Kenner, Hugh. "The Untidy Desk and the Larger Order of Things." *Mazes*, Essays by Hugh Kenner. San Francisco: North Point Press, 1989.

Kline, Mary-Jo. *A Guide to Documentary Editing*, 2nd ed. Baltimore: Johns Hopkins University Press, 1998.

McLean, Renee Troppe. "Take Charge of Every Hour: Ways to Organize Your Time." *Association of Professional Genealogists Quarterly* 7 (June 1992): 38-39.

Mills, Elizabeth Shown. *Evidence! Citation and Analysis for the Family Historian*. Baltimore: Genealogical Publishing Co., 1997.

Rose, Christine. "Protect It We Will: A Professional's Lifetime of Work." *Association of Professional Genealogists Quarterly* 5 (winter 1990): 79-80.

Schlenger, Sunny. *How to Be Organized in Spite of Yourself*. New York: New American Library, 1989.

Schwarz, Ted. *Time Management for Writers*. Cincinnati: Writer's Digest Books, 1988.

Severa, Joan. *Dressed for the Photographer: Ordinary Americans and Fashion*, 1840–1900. Kent, Ohio: Kent State University Press, 1995.

Sibler, Lee. *Time Management for the Creative Person*. New York: Three Rivers Press, 1998.

Stepanek, Marcia. "From Digits to Dust: Surprise—Computer Data Can Decay Before You Know It." *Continental* (August 1998): 27-29. First published in *Business Week* (20 April 1998).

Sturdevant, Katherine Scott. "Documentary Editing for Family Historians." *Association of Professional Genealogists Quarterly* 5 (fall 1990): 51-57.

Summers, Betty. "Business Management for a Family Newsletter." *Association of Professional Genealogists Quarterly* 10 (December 1995): 109-111.

Warren, Paula Stuart, and James W. Warren. "Communicating With Clients Part One: The Information and Rate Sheet." *Association of Professional Genealogists Quarterly* 7 (June 1992): 42-44.

Whitaker, Beverly DeLong. *Beyond Pedigrees: Organizing and Enhancing Your Work*. Salt Lake City: Ancestry, Inc., 1993.

Do You Have Some Organizational or Timesaving Tips?

I would appreciate if you would share your tips with me for the next edition of this book. Also, if you have a question about organizing genealogical materials, a concern about a problem area or a funny story about your organizational blunders, please send them to

Sharon DeBartolo Carmack
P.O. Box 338
Simla, CO 80835
fax: (719) 541-2673
E-mail: sdcarmack@juno.com

Organizational Forms for Genealogists

Sources

Following are blank copies of forms referred to throughout *Organizing Your Family History Search*:

- Note-Taking Form: Couple or Family Group Filing Method (page 134)
- Note-Taking Form: Surname/Type of Record Filing Method (page 135)
- Table of Contents for Files (page 136)
- Correspondence Log—Research Requests (page 137)
- Family Correspondence Log (page 138)
- Research Journal (page 139)
- Research Repository Checklist (page 140)
- Census Checklist (page 141)
- Cemetery Transcription Form (page 142)
- Article Reading List (page 143)
- Book Wish List (page 144)
- Research Checklist of Books (page 145)
- Artifacts and Heirlooms in Other People's Possession (page 146)

These forms are copyright 1999 by Sharon DeBartolo Carmack, but you are free to photocopy them for your *personal* use. No use in a printed work is permitted without permission.

Page _____ of _____

Date _____

NOTE-TAKING FORM
Couple or Family Group Filing Method

Couple _____ **File Number**_____

Type of Record_____

Title/Source_____

Condition of Record_____

Author/Editor/Compiler_____

Publisher_____

Place & Year of Publication_____

Volume_____ Page number_____ Call #/Microfilm # _____

Repository _____

Notes/Abstract

_____
_____
_____
_____
_____
_____
_____
_____
_____
_____
_____
_____
_____
_____
_____
_____
_____
_____
_____
_____
_____

You are free to copy this form for personal use. For instructions on filling it out, see page 16.

Page _____ of _____

Date _____

NOTE-TAKING FORM
Surname/Type of Record Filing Method

Surname _____ Type of Record _____

Title/Source _____

Condition of Record _____

Author/Editor/Compiler _____ _____

Publisher _____

Place & Year of Publication _____

Volume _____ Page number _____ Call #/Microfilm # _____

Repository _____

Notes/Abstract

_____

_____

_____

_____

_____

_____

_____

_____

_____

_____

_____

_____

_____

_____

_____

_____

_____

_____

_____

_____

_____

_____

You are free to copy this form for personal use. For instructions on filling it out, see page 17.

TABLE OF CONTENTS FOR FILES

Surname

Record Type

Enc.#	Date	Listing of Search	Repository/Address	Source Citation	Results	Date Rec'd	Money Sent

You are free to copy this form for personal use. For instructions on filling it out, see page 24.

CORRESPONDENCE LOG
Research Requests

Date	Surname	Name of Ancestor	Record/Information Requested	Repository and Address	Money Sent	Date Rec'd	Results

You are free to copy this form for personal use. For discussion of it, see page 30.

FAMILY CORRESPONDENCE LOG

Surname_____

Date	Correspondence With	Address	Information Rec'd, Sent or Requested

You are free to copy this form for personal use. For discussion of it, see page 31.

RESEARCH JOURNAL

Surname _____

Soundex Code _____

Date	Repository	Source Citation	Objective	Reasoning	Name Variations Checked	Results

You are free to copy this form for personal use. For instructions on filling it out, see page 40.

RESEARCH REPOSITORY CHECKLIST

Name of Repository_____

Address/Directions	
Hours (closed for lunch?)	
Holidays closed	
Name of contact person	
Cost of photocopies	
Restrictions on photocopying	
Change machine or cashier?	
Nearest places to park and cost	
Nearest places to eat	
Local lodging	
Handicap access?	
Research restrictions (Briefcases/laptops allowed? Lockers available and cost?)	
Any records stored off-site? Access?	

You are free to copy this form for personal use. For discussion of it, see page 43.

CENSUS CHECKLIST

Name	1790	1800	1810	1820	1830	1840	1850	1860	1870	1880	1890	1900	1910	1920	1930

You are free to copy this form for personal use. For instructions on filling it out, see page 70.

CEMETERY TRANSCRIPTION FORM

Location of Cemetery:_____

Tombstone Inscription	Tombstone Description
	Headstone: Footstone: Artwork: Grave Decorations:
	Headstone: Footstone: Artwork: Grave Decorations:
	Headstone: Footstone: Artwork: Grave Decorations:
	Headstone: Footstone: Artwork: Grave Decorations:
	Headstone: Footstone: Artwork: Grave Decorations:
	Headstone: Footstone: Artwork: Grave Decorations:
	Headstone: Footstone: Artwork: Grave Decorations:
	Headstone: Footstone: Artwork: Grave Decorations:
	Headstone: Footstone: Artwork: Grave Decorations:

You are free to copy this form for personal use. For instructions on filling it out, see page 72.

ARTICLE READING LIST

Ancestry	*Ancestry* magazine	On Board	Board for Certification of Genealogists Newsletter
APGQ	*Association of Professional Genealogists Quarterly*	Record	*The New York Genealogical and Biographical Record*
FORUM	*Federation of Genealogical Societies FORUM*	Register	*The New England Historical and Genealogical Register*
GC	*Genealogical Computing*		
GJ	*Genealogical Journal*	TAG	*The American Genealogist*
Helper	*Genealogical Helper*	TG	*The Genealogist*
HQ	*Heritage Quest*		
NEXUS	New England Historic Genealogical Society Newsletter		
NGSQ	*National Genealogical Society Quarterly*		
NGSN	National Genealogical Society Newsletter		

Article Title or Topic	Journal/Newsletter	Issue

You are free to copy this form for personal use. For discussion of it, see page 87.

BOOK WISH LIST

ANC	Ancestry	NEHGS	New England Historic Genealogical Soc.
BW	Betterway Books	SHP	Southern Historical Press
EP	Everton Publishers	VB	Virginia Book Co.
FP	Frontier Press	_____	_____
GPC	Genealogical Publishing Co.	_____	_____
HSB	Hearthstone Books	_____	_____
HB	Heritage Books	_____	_____

Title	Author's Last Name	Catalog & Page	Price

You are free to copy this form for personal use. For discussion of it, see page 88.

RESEARCH CHECKLIST OF BOOKS

Title	Author	Surnames to Check

You are free to copy this form for personal use. For discussion of it, see page 88.

ARTIFACTS AND HEIRLOOMS IN OTHER PEOPLE'S POSSESSION

Date	Identification of Artifact and Its Condition	In Whose Possession (Name, Address, Phone)	To Whom It Will Be Passed (Name, Address, Phone)

You are free to copy this form for personal use. For discussion of it, see page 122.

Index